THAT MAN IS YOU

THAT MAN IS YOU

BY LOUIS EVELY

TRANSLATED BY EDMOND BONIN

PAULIST PRESS

New York/Ramsey/Toronto

Nihil obstat: JOHN F. DEDE, S.S., J.C.D.
Censor Deputatus

Imprimatur: LAWRENCE J. SHEHAN, D.D.
Archbishop of Baltimore

April 8, 1963

TRANSLATOR'S NOTE

The text of this translation has been disposed in sense
lines, not to create the illusion of verse (indeed, there is far
more truth than poetry in these hard-hitting pages—unless
such truth be the highest poetry), but to facilitate meditation. Based on the ancient method of printing prose *per cola
et commata*, this sense-line arrangement throws into greater
relief the development, co-ordination and subordination of
ideas, emphasizes significant parallelism and antithesis, and
permits one to isolate key words.

The notes will be found after Chapter Nine. Mostly refer-
ences to the Bible, they should almost all be preceded by the
abbreviation *cf.*, since few are exact quotations. *Abbé* Evely
has a gift for abridging, telescoping or expanding Scriptural
texts so as to bring out their latent meaning; as his concern
is pastoral rather than exegetical, he judiciously updates the
diction and even uses anachronisms to prove the timelessness
of God's word. I have, therefore, found it necessary to work
out a new translation—or, rather, paraphrase—of the Scriptural passages, because the English versions now available
would clash with the author's direct, down-to-earth style, and
because I am convinced that Jesus spoke to Palestine's fisher-
men and farmers and housewives and soldiers in the language
they understood, and not in some wooden, pseudo-solemn
phraseology. Did not Mary address Bernadette, the children
of La Salette and the seers of Fatima in their own dialects?

E. B.

PREFACE

There is a Pomeranian proverb to the effect that goats will devour anything fresh and green. After observing some of my Belgian friends, I surmised that they had found such nourishment for their soul. Still, I knew that, like the rest of their generation, they felt the need of going back to the sources, getting to the bottom of questions and settling for nothing short of the truth. What, then, had they discovered? Like the first disciples of old, they had met someone who spoke to them of God; or, like the Samaritan woman, they had heard a voice that said, "If only you knew the gift of God!" Like the two pilgrims from Emmaus, they had felt their heart catch fire as someone explained the Scriptures to them and finished revealing himself in the way he broke bread.

They introduced me to him: a young priest from the diocese of Malines, the director of the Collège Cardinal Mercier at Braine-l'Alleud. *Abbé* Evely—for it was he—is well known in Belgium as a retreat master, a radio and television speaker, the guiding spirit behind family organizations, and a contributor to *Témoignage chrétien* and *Revue nouvelle*. A short time ago, Editions Fleurus of Paris published the text of an unforgettable retreat he had preached to a group of families on the mutual connection between the fatherhood of God and the brotherhood of man.

I, too, read *Notre Père: Aux sources de notre Fraternité*. Like all *abbé* Evely's hearers and readers, I was struck, first of all, by his "tone." Far different from sheer style, and far more important, that "tone" consists in retelling the message of Christ with vigor. *Abbé* Evely has a knack of making us perceive the full import, spiritual and human, of the truths we thought we understood and of making us see them from a different angle, under irrecusable light, as when a naughty child suddenly finds his mother looking at him. The power to help others discover the old, familiar sources in a fresh, new way is certainly a gift granted to those who loyally serve the kingdom of God, bringing forth "new things and old."[1] A good Scribe, *abbé* Evely knows how to set the precious stones of the kingdom of heaven. He makes the Gospels come to life, so that we often seem to be hearing or reading them for the first time. With such pages ringing in my ears, I cannot help feeling somewhat like a lexicographer who has been asked to introduce a poet. Poets speak for themselves!

If cultivated artificially and for its own sake, "tone" can neither nourish souls nor change lives. Young people—especially today—detest rhetoric but respond when candidly shown a clear, consistent ideal that entails certain renunciations and eventually imposes difficult standards. Without watering down the consequences, *abbé* Evely presents the facts about God, His fatherhood and His Word, about Christ and His Holy Spirit, as a philosophy of life which, ultimately, holds together only if we fully accept its paradox: the paradox of our faith.

The faith did not begin with the present generation any

more than the Church did. As we study the tide of ideas which we have ridden on in the last twenty-five years, we notice, first and foremost, the break with the past and the novelty of the themes; we are struck by the discoveries or the rediscoveries. But the more we know and think, the better we see how closely successive eras are bound together and to what extent each young generation is borne by its elders, who, in turn, owe everything to those who preceded them. Newman has written on this subject with the Christian humility and the serene and optimistic equipoise that characterize his thought.[2] We are always building on the foundations others have laid and reaping the fruits of what others have sown.[3]

When we consider the general course of religion in the last hundred and thirty years or so, we cannot but view it as a reconquest and a gradual restoration of Christianity, rising on the ruins of that ancient "Christian society" which was overthrown by the ideological, political, economic and social revolution at the end of the eighteenth and the beginning of the nineteenth century. In a certain way, this progressive re-establishment meant reintegrating Christian society itself —not its mere structure, but its soul; it meant rediscovering, in a world that was growing ever more profane, the Christian specific and, to be precise, the faith. The more this world becomes secular and even reverts to a sort of paganism, the more do Christians go back to the faith for revitalization.

That involves far more than adopting the familiar, stereotyped attitudes of a sociological Catholicism, along with "religious" customs inherited from our milieu the way we inherit social standing and corresponding obligations and modes of behavior. It even goes much deeper than those "practices" and "devotions" which never amount to more than a ready-made "religion." Instead, it requires a complete surrender of self—of a living person—to the living God. Christianity, we must be thoroughly convinced, is anything but an established "religious" society. We live in the world and, while here, must try to comport ourselves like Christians; but, as such, we are not of the world: because of our faith, we belong to the kingdom of heaven, whose ruler is Jesus. Today's Christians—not only individually and in their personal interior piety, but collectively and as a Church—have once again become more aware of the eschatological character of Christianity and of the exigencies of the faith.

We have participated in the successive stages of this rediscovery. Inspired by the efforts of the liturgical revival, by the deeply apostolic generosity of the *"Génération d'Agathon"** (whose best representatives were mowed down on the battle-fields of World War I), and by the genuinely prophetic words of Pius XI as he organized Catholic Action, we have, first of all, gained a clearer understanding of the mystery of the Mystical Body. We have returned to the sources for our ideas on the Church and sacramental life, which is entirely centered in Christ and, ultimately, in His passage through this world.

Today, we are on the threshold of a new stage in our series of rediscoveries. The role of Holy Scripture in this last phase is fairly well recognized. God's people have once more developed a hunger for this bread without which they cannot live;*

---

* *"Agathon"* was the joint pseudonym of Henri Massis and Alfred de Tarde, journalists and critics who, in 1911, published the results of two surveys on the intellectual, moral and religious temper of pre-war French youth, and, by eloquently voicing its ideals and steadily elevating them, contributed in no small measure to the rebirth of militant Catholicism.—Tr.

they want it to impart its flavor to preaching and catechesis, because they understand that, without it, they cannot evangelize the world or themselves, as the Christian apostolate always must and as so many in our day ardently long to do.

> My soul thirsts for God, for the living God. . . .
> Day and night, I have no bread but my tears
> as men ceaselessly taunt, "Where is your God?"[5]

The faithful who have relearned to live in the communion of Abraham and Moses, of the book of Exodus, the prophets and the Psalms; who have heard the Gospels' total call to practice the Beatitudes, to give of self and bear witness; and who devote themselves to filling the world with acts inspired by these imperatives—such persons need, more than ever, to know and pray the God of faith: not the God proposed by some Stoic philosophy, however noble it may be; not the God who crowns some rationalistic or politico-religious system, but the God of faith—the God of Abraham, in a word, the God of Exodus, of the Psalms and Christian prayer, the Father of our Lord Jesus Christ. In short, it seems that the liturgical and ecclesiastical renewal, thanks to which we have a better comprehension of the Mystical Body and of Easter, must now be climaxed by a Biblical renewal that would deepen and clarify the very notion of God as the God of our belief and our prayer. This is also necessary if the activity and testimony of Christians working in the world is to have its full effect; it must not be the mere product of an inherited religion, but must perpetually spring from the faith and from obedience to the God of faith. My God—the God of my belief and my prayer—calls and makes demands, scrutinizes me and says, "That man is you!"

As I read *Notre Père: Aux sources de notre Fraternité* and parts of the present book in manuscript, I felt that *abbé* Evely's message satisfies these needs quite remarkably. Many have already heeded it because it contains what they require and because they have found there some of the absolute exigency and paradox of that Christianity which is also the Christianity of faith, to which they were drawn.

His doctrine may appear too uniformly taut and demanding, too constantly extreme and sublime. He seems to be asking for a perpetual miracle, unflagging heroism. But that is what the Gospels do. "This is a hard saying . . ."[6] And after many a paragraph, like after each verse of *The Imitation of Christ*, we cannot help saying, "This is terribly exacting but absolutely right."

Perhaps the Christian paradox, which so easily lends itself to admirable poetry, is expressed here (I refer to *Notre Père: Aux sources de notre Fraternité*) with an enthusiasm or triumphant optimism that the difficulties and failures of life do not completely justify. I am thinking of Pierre Schaeffer's *Enfants de coeur*, the disillusioned cry of one who had taken the sublime poetry of Christianity literally. I am thinking, also, of a man whose little girl had died and who said of Claudel's *L'Annonce faite à Marie*, "That isn't how things happen in real life!" There are sufferings and unfortunate situations that the preacher of the Christian paradox must approach with respect, presenting his message with the greatest humility like a man who is himself weak and crushed, making room everywhere for arduous effort and defeat, showing the dimension of the Cross in the Christian life and the need for the kind of faith, hope and struggle that go on even in the darkness of night. A string that is too steadily stretched may snap. All will agree that his purpose is, not to discourage his hearers and lower them in their own estimation, but to demonstrate the transcendency and the absoluteness of the Christian paradox in all its realism. In order to do so, he must foresee the possibility of problems and sin, wait patiently as God's mercy does, echo the serene simplicity of the Gospels, acknowledge unsuccess and human limitations, and even have a sense of humor. For humor—the nickname of wisdom—is not absent from the lives of the saints. We have only to recall Saint Philip Neri, who used to pray each morning, "Protect me from myself, O Lord; I could very well be a Mohammedan before the day's over." Indeed, there is in each of us a pagan, a Jew and a Christian. Here below, the Christian life consists, not so much in being a Christian, but in trying to become one as best we can.

To that end, it is good that we have an echo of God's word to call and reprove us continually. I remember how often I have felt tempted to relax after a period of intense spiritual endeavor—after a retreat, for example, or after experiencing grace and light. At such times, I wondered, "Won't I be allowed to enjoy myself a little? Or will I always be forced, from now on, to do the most perfect thing, the most difficult? Will I have to keep giving all the time and never take anything back for myself?" But no one whom God has really worked upon can ever again be content with mediocrity. "Your words have stuck fast within me": I could not tear out of my flesh the dart God's word had left there. As Ben Arabi says, "The man whose sickness is called 'Jesus' can never be cured." Accordingly, from the very depth of the cowardice or weakness that reared its head within me, a voice rang out, all the stronger for its being so fragile: "O Lord, don't forsake me; don't give me a moment's rest. Keep talking to me, I beg You; keep calling, keep asking more and more. . . ."

And as for this book, I pray, "Let it, too, be for many readers a transcription of Your voice and Your will!"

YVES M.-J. CONGAR, O.P.

Cambridge
On the feast of Saint Francis of Assisi
1956

CONTENTS

ONE: IS GOD REALLY SILENT?

Would we have recognized Christ?
>How?
So many of those He met during His earthly life didn't.
And we—why would we have recognized Him?
>Why would we have failed to?

"Oh," we exclaim, "if we'd lived in His day,
>if we could've heard
>>and seen
>>>and touched Him,
how dearly we'd have loved Him,
how gladly we'd have left everything to follow Him!"

Really?
Haven't we ever seen or touched Him?
>We can commune with Him every day. . . .
We never hear Him?
>He's there every day,
>>waiting to speak to us in the Gospels. . .
We've never met Him?
>"I was hungry, and you fed Me.
>I was thirsty.
>I was a stranger. . . ."[1]

Not a moment passes but we fail to see Him
>in one of our neighbors.

"I'm with you every day,
       even till the end of the world."[2]
   Could we have received greater strength,
                         stronger assurance,
                         tenderer care?
   He's with us "every single day."

Nothing's further from the truth
   than the nostalgia that makes people imagine
       they'd have been good Christians
           if only they'd lived two thousand years ago.

On the contrary,
   it's quite probable that our vices,
       instead of melting away at His approach,
   would've kept us from acknowledging Him,
       as happened to the thousands and thousands
           who drew near out of curiosity
               and slipped away disillusioned
                   at finding Him so ordinary,
                               insufferably eccentric
                               and even scandalous.
"Blessed is he who isn't scandalized in Me."[3]

It's the same all over again
   every morning.
Christ doesn't change,
   and neither do men.
The Gospels are full of revelations:
       revelations about God
           and revelations about ourselves.

They tell us the story of Jesus
    in His meetings with men—
        all sorts of men,
        all sorts of meetings—
    as He was in the beginning,
        is now
        and ever shall be.
They show us how God's always treated men
        and how men mistreat Him.

"And so," we muse, "Jesus could be near us for years
    without our knowing it?"
The truth is that not a day has passed
    but we've met Him.
    How often have we welcomed Him?
    How often have we failed to recognize Him,
    how often slighted or condemned Him?
We mustn't think those people in the Gospels
        who tortured Christ
    were worse than we.
They were full of good intentions.
Like us, they didn't realize what they were doing.
    They thought they were promoting the common good;
    they were following their conscience;
    they executed Christ
        because their "right" conscience told them to.
Just like us. . . .
And Jesus prayed, "Father, forgive them,
    for they don't know what they're doing."[4]
"In your midst there has stood someone you don't know."[5]
    This admonition of Saint John the Baptist's

is also a living word,
a judgment that keeps re-echoing,
a prophecy for all time.
"In your midst . . ." for how many years now?
Jesus'd been living among His own for thirty years:
He'd met them a hundred times,
worked with them,
done them favors,
looked at them,
listened and spoken to them,
and no one'd paid any attention to Him—
for thirty years.

Yes, this admonition's a living word
and it concerns each and every one of us.
Between Him and us hangs the same veil,
the same screen
of indifference
and querulous hostility.
Deep down, each of us is violently opposed to the divine.
With all our might we reject this God
who dares differ so outrageously
from the notion we'd formed of Him.

Still stronger and more startling than John's indictment
are Jesus' words to Philip on the eve of His Passion.
After three years of public life,
manifesting Himself each day,
teaching at every moment
and living in their midst,
He was obliged to upbraid

one of those He'd shared His whole adventure with.
"Philip, I've been with you so long,
and you don't know Me yet!"[6]

After twenty centuries
is there one of us He couldn't say the same thing to?
"It's been such a long time . . . and still you don't know Me.
You haven't yet understood
that I'm hungry
and thirsty
and poor;
that I was where you found
nothing to honor or admire,
nothing to fear or reverence;
that I was precisely where you felt so sure
I couldn't be."

After two thousand years of public life,
the presence of God is still a hidden one;
and it always will be.
Only when we give up fashioning Him in our image
and seeking Him
where we think He should be—
only then will we perceive it.
God's most insistent call to us
will always seem a sort of silence,
since His language isn't what we expect.
Only when we love Him enough
to prefer His ways to ours,
His language

and His will—
only then will we discover Him.

Even when Jesus appeared after His Resurrection,
no one knew Him right away.
Whenever God manifests Himself,
He's always unknown and unrecognized at first.
The disciples of Emmaus walked a good way,
listened
and warmed their hearts
in His presence
for a long time
without realizing who was comforting them.
They recognized Him, at last,
in the breaking of the bread.
On the edge of Lake Tiberias,
the Apostles' net had to be miraculously filled
to the snapping point
before one of them—
"the disciple Jesus loved"[7]—
finally cried out:
"It's the Lord!"
But Mary Magdalene,
confused enough to mistake Christ for the gardener,
knew Him the moment He spoke her name.

"He who is of God hears His words."[8]
If we patiently and perseveringly try to understand
the things of God,
we'll gradually learn to recognize
His voice.

We bemoan God's "silence," His absence;
we like to picture our joy on seeing Him glorified
        at last
          by some event or other.
Still, He's as truly with us
         as He was with His contemporaries,
and Scripture tells us
      they were just as unaware of His presence
          as we are.

Are we simple-hearted and credulous enough to believe
        that the Word became flesh *for us* also,
        that He dwells among us
          and that we're the ones who ceaselessly reject Him,
        that He wants only to live with us
          and that we're the ones who haven't welcomed Him?
"He came to His own, and His own didn't receive Him."[9]
"Men have loved the darkness rather than the light,
         for their works were evil."[10]
Are we honest enough to admit
        that *there* lies the cause of the gloom
         which seems to surround us?
"The light shines in the darkness"[11]—in our darkness.

For thousands of years
        the Jewish people'd been prepared, educated,
                    admonished and trained
         to receive the Messias.
    He came, and they failed to welcome Him. . . .
Now, they were men who believed
         in their Scribes, their doctors of the law,

their theologians, pastors and parents;
they'd learned their religion well
and could quote its tenets at the drop of a skull cap.
They were God's chosen people,
specialists in matters of religion,
experts in all that concerned Him;
and God was with them,
but they didn't notice Him.
"Lord," they thought, "that's not
how You were supposed to appear!
Can anything good come out of Nazareth?[12]
It's all very well to do the unexpected,
but there's a limit.
We've learned—
in fact, we've read—
all sorts of things
that You just don't conform to."

As for us modern Israelites,
let's beware of so perfecting the formulas of dogma
that we lose interest in its content.
Let's beware of studying the signs so assiduously
that we forget the reality they signify.
Let's beware lest, having believed so long,
our faith be dulled;
lest, having awaited Christ so long,
our expectancy be blunted.

Do we believe in God—
or in those who've spoken to us about Him?

Believing in God presupposes,
    not that we've acquired notions or data
                  about religious experience,
    but that we've met a person—
              a living person;
it implies a drawing near,
        a contact,
        a conversion
        and a reaching out.
    All those who've met Jesus professed some kind of religion:
        they all believed in the God they'd been told about.
But those who've followed Jesus
        have had to reject the ideas
                they so laboriously acquired
            and replace them
                by His own very different ideas.
The most painful conversion of all
    is the one each of us has to effect
        at the very heart of his religion.

From the first step,
    those who've followed Jesus
        have had to revise their concept of God
                and, therefore, break with everything
        that imbued them with it:
            friends, connections, social milieu
            and the entire conventional framework
                    of ideas and practices
            that Jesus came to turn inside out.
We have to abandon the whole worm-eaten structure
                that Christ came to blow up—

abandon it immediately, utterly—
when we follow Jesus,
when we start believing in God,
in the true God,
in the living God.

When someone starts believing for good,
when he starts taking God seriously once for all,
he usually begins by scandalizing everybody:
all those "good Christians" who are too "humble"
to depart from the accepted pattern;
all those who feel they have the right religion—
a time-honored one that jolts nobody.

Take Saint Paul, for example,
when he was persecuting the Christians.[13]
He thought he had the right religion.
None was more cognizant of its commands than he,
none more zealous in having them carried out.
He'd become furious with people
who were forever questioning everything
and who seemed to think
some matters hadn't been definitively settled yet.
"After all," he reasoned, "we have the Law.
Everything's been foreseen and legislated.
Let's not have any of these innovations!"
He was a strict observer of complete orthodoxy.
Still, when this thoroughly religious man
finally and really met the God
he thought he was serving,

he was thunderstruck
            and gasped, "Who—who are you?"[14]
The God he'd so fiercely clung to had hardened into an idol.

How about our God,
            the one we think we're serving?
Is He the tender,
                solicitous,
                responsive,
                persecuted—
                and, therefore, persecutable—being
        who revealed Himself to Saint Paul?
Or is He some almighty, remote bookkeeper
        who'll catch us the next time around
            if our accounts aren't in order?
Many Christians wouldn't want to be the God
                they've fabricated:
        they'd be more likeable than that!

When Jesus revealed Himself
                and, consequently, the Father
        (for "he who sees Me sees the Father also"[15]),
we discovered, first of all, that God's infinitely better
                than we'd imagined.
    He's near us,
            benevolent,
            young and gay,
            companionable and loving.
    He begs for our friendship:
        if we wander away from Him,

[13]

He runs after us in the thorns and brambles;
if we stray from home,
He watches for us till we've come back;
and when we do,
He's overflowing with tenderness
and just can't do enough to celebrate our return.[16]

Well, then, if we've never met him,
whose fault is it—
His or ours?
Throughout the Bible, God's own word proclaims
that it's He who seeks out man,
from Genesis:
"Where are you, Adam?"[17]
to the Apocalypse:
"Listen! I stand at the door and knock.
If anyone hears My voice and opens the door,
I'll come in and eat with him,
and he'll eat with Me."[18]
He knocks constantly,
"like that exasperating shutter
which sometimes keeps pounding and hammering
till dawn,
or like the old door
we thought we'd blocked up for good.
Someone has knocked within us, and we're annoyed:
what a nuisance to have to get up and unseal that door!
Still, someone has knocked—God.
And, always and everywhere,
He finds only that hard, unyielding wall.
O Lord, we'll try to open our hearts to You,

for we know You don't enjoy striking us."[19]

Pascal's God declares,
    "You wouldn't be seeking Me
      if you hadn't already found Me."
    Shouldn't He rather say,
    ". . . if I hadn't already found you"?
God can be forgotten,
        repudiated,
        abandoned
        and betrayed,
      but He's always and forever a saviour,
                          a faithful friend,
                          a father.
    He can't change:
      a son may stop being a son,
      but the Father can never stop being a father.
Man's hunger for God is nothing
          compared to God's hunger for man.
God never fails to keep rendezvous with man;
    in fact, He arranges them.
No one's ever sought Him
    without finding Him.
No one can say he put himself at God's disposal
    without hearing and meeting Him,
    without being acted upon,
          cured and consoled,
          moved and snatched up.

God's no more ceased being Revelation

than He's ceased being Love.
He didn't love us just once,
                    incidentally,
                         two thousand years ago.
Love must express and communicate itself.
    That's its nature.
    When people begin to love one another,
        they start telling everything that's happened to them,
                     every detail of their daily life;
        they "reveal" themselves to each other,
            unbosom themselves and exchange confidences.

God continually reaches out toward us
            to share secrets
                we continually refuse to hear.
    It's He who wants to manifest Himself
        and we who are too flighty,
                    too preoccupied,
                    too mistrustful,
                    too hostile.
We obstinately resist God
        by hiding under layers of distraction and indifference,
                    repugnance and antagonism.
But every desire we have for Him
    and every prayer
        is like the stroke of a scrub plane
            that thins down our wooden-hearted incredulity;
and when we've prayed enough
    and the boards are worn quite through,
        we'll realize God was there all the while,

waiting patiently,
pressing hard to set us free.

Prayer alone can wear down our frightful resistance to God.
Praying is exposing ourselves to His influence,
placing ourselves under His command
so that He may do in us for once
what He'd want to do forever,
giving Him, at last, time and opportunity
to entrust Himself and His secrets to us,
as He's planned from eternity.
Praying is letting Him kill in us
that boorish, loud-mouthed, egotistic character
whose bellowing keeps us from conversing with God.
Making a retreat means bringing ourselves to understand
that the trouble doesn't lie with God,
that it's we who've been untrue
and forgetful
and heedless,
we who've been indifferent
and unrelenting.
But to see the truth that clearly
and go beneath the unruffled surface
(where we've been careful to stay
so as to protect ourselves,
keep the true God from being God
in us
and muffle the importunate,
loving call
we dread answering)—

to do that,
we have to pray long,
calmly
and with inward attention.

A Trappist friend of mine used to say,
"It's not enough to apply the brakes on your car;
you must also cut the motor that's racing inside."
The engine of our solicitudes is still whirring at top speed.
It has to slacken,
decelerate
and turn at an easier pace.
We have to move in time with another rhythm,
gear our will to another will,
learn to connect with the slow-paced,
quiet,
powerful
and steady motor
of God's will.

As long as we're in a turmoil,
taken up with our problems and our interests,
we're safely sheltered from God
and out of His reach.
We need several days of recollection
before we can begin to live in Him
and on Him.
We have to stay there in a kind of stupor
and let our motor idle
till we've adjusted to a new tempo
we've never experienced before.

If we're too intent on our questions,
    we can't hear God's answers,
        which are surprising,
            disconcerting,
            and never come to us the way we expect.
To meet God, we have to get away from ourselves.
    Retreatants always stuff their suitcase with a pile of things:
            letters to be answered,
            a book,
            three or four chocolate bars,
            a newspaper
            and a train schedule
                in case the whole business becomes
                    intolerable.
We all feel the need of a few projects
    to shield us from God.
We imagine He can't nourish us.
What we must do, instead, is disencumber ourselves—
            even of major problems,
            even vital ones.
He'll discuss all that with us
        in His own good time
        and in His own way.
    It's none of our business,
                but His;
    it's His worry
            far more than ours.

We're all panting and puffing under a burden that's unbearable
    because we've taken it on ourselves without authorization.

Once more, God must become God for us, .
                        regain His proper place
                             and His rights.
    When we've let Him do that,
        we'll be enormously relieved;
        we'll try to remember
                how we could ever attach so much importance
                                to matters
                            that concerned only *us*,
                since now,
                    in relation to God,
                    we find ourselves so insignificant.
    When we've placed our burden
                    on the only shoulders that can take it,
        we'll discover that it's light and bearable
                        and that we have what we need
                                to carry it.

May God become God for us once again!
Let's allow Him to be for us what He really is:
                        all love and thoughtfulness,
                        our vocation and our reward;
let's allow Him at last to show us His true face,
    instead of the dark, joyless mask we've painted Him.
        He invites us every day
                to this illuminating discovery,
                    this transfiguration.

One of the Fathers of the Church suggests that it wasn't Christ
        who was changed and transformed on Mount Tabor.
    A supernatural glow emanated from His face

the whole time He was with His Apostles,
but their eyes were kept from seeing Him as He was.
One day, Peter, James and John followed Him
to a solitary spot—
a craggy, silent mountain,
far from the crowds
where they usually acted so important and officious,
like influential mediators.
Now, on the peaceful mountaintop,
they gradually composed themselves,
started seeing things in perspective
and became attentive to Him;
so that,
taken up with Him alone
and open to His influence,
they unsealed their eyes and beheld Him
for a moment
as He really was all the time.[20]

Do we want to see Jesus and His glory?
Do we want Him to manifest Himself
and be transfigured before us?
Then, we should devote a morning to Him
or spend an evening in church
or a whole afternoon
in a beautiful tree-girt meadow
with only the Gospels for company.
If we do that,
we can expect
(and if we've already done so, we know)
that, bit by bit,

in the hush of the chapel
or the stillness of nature,
our eyes'll slowly open
and we'll start seeing ourselves and Him
very clearly.
We'll discover what we're now hiding—
the evil we do,
whether we're aware of it
or whether we refuse to advert to it.
We'll hear His voice,
those words He's always speaking to us
but which we try so hard not to hear.
We'll see plainly what He wants of us.
His presence will become so real and immediate
that it may oppress us somewhat;
His radiant face, more magnetic
than anything we've ever known.
Like so many others before us, we, too, will say,
"Lord, it's good to be here!
Oh, if I could always be like this and never change. . . .
Let me pitch my tent here and stay forever."[31]

Why this joy?
Because, at long last, we'll have discovered
that the Lord,
though hidden and unnoticed,
was with us all the time.
"In your midst there has stood someone you don't know."[22]

TWO: *GOD'S WORD IS A LIVING THING*

Saint Paul exclaims,
  "God's word is a living thing!"[1]
Living—
     that means
  it's actual,
     being spoken at this very moment,
     continually and tirelessly repeated,
     born again in God's heart every day
         to be transmitted to living men,
  and it's always fresh,
              new for each and every man,
              personal,
              meant to illuminate him individually.
This word's "the true light that enlightens everyone
         who comes into the world."[2]
There's not a soul on earth God doesn't speak to.

The keenest suffering and the bitterest complaint
              of modern unbelievers
  arise from the "silence of God,"
     against which they seem to bang their head
     whenever they try, in all sincerity, to look for Him.
"After all," replies the doctor in Camus' *La Peste*,
     "since the order of the world is dominated by death,
     perhaps it's better for God that we don't believe in Him
     but war against death for all we're worth,

without looking up to heaven,
where He sits perfectly silent."
What answer do we have to this despair?
Are we convinced He's spoken to us?
Do we believe wholeheartedly in His living word,
in that ever-present voice
which keeps uttering,
for each of us,
the words that can heal?
"Say but the word . . ."[8]

Our faith in God's word is measured by our faith in His love.
We don't really believe He speaks to us
because we don't really believe He loves us.
What's a saint?
It's someone who believes that God loves him.
"We've come to know and believe in God's love for us."[4]
Anyone who believes God loves him
knows that God speaks to him.

God hasn't ceased being Revelation
any more than He's ceased being Love.
He enjoys expressing Himself.
Since He's Love,
He must give Himself,
share His secrets,
communicate with us
and reveal Himself to anyone
who wants to listen.
His sole delight is to confide in us
and give Himself to us.

God's revelation began with Adam in the Garden of Eden.
(There, too, began the Passion.
Don't we say,
when someone trusts us,
that he's put himself in our hands?)
He'd come into the Garden in the cool of the evening
and talk to Adam as a friend.[5]
He was starting to manifest Himself
and share His thoughts,
trying to make us understand who He is
and delivering Himself up to us.
And, from the outset, He was shunned and rejected.
"His own didn't receive Him."[6]
From the beginning, from the first day,
Adam interrupted the dialogue,
scorned God's confidences
and shattered the alliance they gave proof of.
From the very start,
it was man who walked away,
man who turned a deaf ear to God's words.
The Passion began in Paradise.

But God's never wearied of talking to us.
He keeps reopening the conversation,
hoping we'll listen;
He keeps offering His friendship,
however often we spurn Him.
In the desert, He used to visit Moses in his tent
and speak to him
"face to face, as a man speaks to his friend."[7]
"And after having spoken to our fathers through the prophets

[27]

on many occasions and in many ways,
God has at last, in our day, spoken to us through His Son."[8]

His communications'd grown so urgent,
He'd given and entrusted His word to us so completely,
and He'd reached out toward man so far
that the Word, His utterance, became flesh.
The Incarnation was God's crowning prophecy,
His supreme attempt to reveal Himself.
He'd created flesh
and he so ardently wanted it to accept
and understand Him
that He became flesh Himself.
He took the word
which He'd never been able to transmit to us
without our garbling or forgetting it,
voiced it fully
and made it man.
God doesn't repent His gifts.
He placed His word in our hands
and has never taken it back.
Once and for all, He came down to the level of each of us;
He became flesh
so we could eat Him in His sacrament,
love Him in our neighbor
and hear and follow Him
in the Gospels.

Those Gospels are God's message directed to every one of us.
We must believe that God inspired the Evangelists
in such a way

that their words were really dictated by Him.
Are we truly aware of that when we open our Bible?
    Yet that's what the charism
        of scriptural inspiration means.
If God's the author,
    how can He fail to move us directly
        every time we take up His Book
                and expose ourselves to His influence?
"The Holy Spirit'll teach you whatever I've said to you."[9]
    This promise, made shortly before Jesus' death, indicates
        that the words He spoke once
            will have to be studied constantly
        and that He said all of them
            while He was in the world
            precisely so that the Spirit might expound them
                till the end of the world.
The Holy Spirit forever conveys to those words
                a new impulse
                and a vital power
                    aimed at our heart.
    "I'll speak to her heart."[10]

Many people say—and goodness knows how many
                more believe—
    that some revelation took place
                        in the dim past
                    and is now preserved
                        in the Church's deposit
                            of faith.
    They admit there was a contact,
                an utterance,

a living communication—
for others;
but, as for us, all we have left is a "deposit,"
a residue,
to be guarded vigilantly.

What a shameful view!
Is that what we think of God's love for us?
Is that how we conceive
"the things He's prepared for those
who love Him"?[11]

The letter kills.
Only the Spirit gives life,
because He's alive.
When we read a passage in God's Book,
we must think of it,
not as a text to be perused
or an idea to be dissected,
but as God Himself coming into our tent
to speak to us face to face
as a man speaks to his friend.
If we listened to Him in this frame of mind,
His word would be "living and operative"[12] in us;
it'd produce results,
cure us
and raise us up from the dead.
If we received it as it's given us,
this living word would nourish us all day long
just as the living bread does at Mass in the morning.
After celebrating the Eucharist,
the Orthodox Churches don't reserve the Blessed

Sacrament
on the altar
but place the Gospels there
between two candles.

Sustained by His Body,
we're ready to "hear God's word and keep it"[13]
and to let ourselves be prepared thus—
by His efficacious word
and our fidelity to it—
for our next Communion.

The communion God offers us with Himself is uninterrupted;
and the conversation He'd hold with us, inexhaustible.
He speaks to us constantly;
or, rather, calls us constantly:
"Hello! Don't hang up. I want to talk to you. . . ."
And we—are we all ears,
breathlessly eager to hear the Lord?
He speaks to us
and wants to all the time,
from where He lives.
"But you've given Me neither heed nor hearing."[14]

"He who is of God hears His words."[15]
To hear that incessant call and be moved and nurtured by it,
the reader needs the same grace of inspiration
the Evangelists had.
God's the only one who can talk about God adequately
and listen properly.
"No one knows the Father except the Son."[16]
To know God,

we have to become God;
we have to become sons in the Son
in order to recognize our Father's voice.
He doesn't manifest Himself on our terms.
The first thing He told Abraham was,
"Leave all this behind and come away."[17]
To see God,
we have to become God.
And that hurts:
we must be willing
to die
(for "no mortal can see God and live"[18]),
to forego all sorts of things
without which life seems impossible,
to be thoroughly tested,
slowly stripped of ourselves,
dispossessed,
driven from our last hiding place,
from the final inch of solid ground
we dreamed of resting
our feet on,
forced to believe
rather than know,
to hope
rather than have,
to love
without fanfare,
without reserve
and without guarantees,
to be a mere longing,
though our every instinct and dream

                        clamors
                for permanence and security,
                ownership, control and certitude.

C. S. Lewis compares the painful process of divinizing man
        to domesticating a dog.
By nature, dogs are wild, predatory, snappish,
                        dirty and intractable.
If we want to train them to live with human beings
                and impart to them some of our human
                                reactions,
        we have to correct and whip them
                and teach them to keep clean and not run off
                        with everything they find.
All this seems counter to their nature, but,
        thanks to the permanent contradiction we effect,
they're eventually capable of affection,
                                faithfulness
                                and sociability—
        qualities we'd never have thought
                they could acquire.
Their fidelity is so touching,
they're so content in our company
                and appear so overjoyed and thrilled
        with the human traits we've communicated to them
        that we wonder whether it isn't more natural for them
                        to be men
                        than dogs.
The most unpleasant moments of their training—
        when they stood in a soapy tub,
                trembling with fear and cold and loathing—

seem inconsequential
compared to the new world of enjoyment
their humanization's opened up to them.

It's the same in our relations with God.
The transformation He achieves in us is excruciating, too,
and, through all those baptisms we have to undergo
so as to enter into His life,
we often feel as miserable and helpless and tremulous
as Mr. Lewis' dogs in their tub.
And, still, when we read the lives of the saints
and see the miracles of fidelity and trust
God elicited from them,
their total gift of self,
their innocence
and their joy,
we forget all their trials
and are tempted to think it was more natural for them
to be God
than men.

No one can see God and yet live.
It's impossible to know Him
and not change,
to recognize Him
and not love Him above all else,
impossible to be transformed
without first losing
what we think is our essential
form,
to be transfigured

without first being disfigured
in our own sight.

God won't appear to us on our level:
> fickle as we are,
> cross-grained and selfish,
> proud, ambitious and independent.

We'll understand Him only if we speak His language.
> Suppose a man turns on his short-wave radio
> > with no particular program in mind,
> > twirls the dial this way and that
> > and picks up a foreign-language program
> > he doesn't understand at all for a while.

"Let's see. Is that English? Of course not!
> French? No.
> Italian, maybe. . . . Yes, that's it—Italian!"

From the instant he consents not to listen in English
> > but orients himself to this other language,
> > agrees to this uprooting
> > and adjusts to transplantation,
> everything becomes intelligible and full of meaning.

But as long as he thinks it's English,
> he doesn't catch a bit of the message.

God speaks within us all the time
> and has been doing so right along
> > in His own language—
> the simple, sober language of everyday life.

We don't understand Him
> because we're waiting for Him to use ours—
> > a make-believe lingo of happiness

(as we fancy it)
to gratify our poor, stupid sentimentality,
to flatter our self-love
and even comfort us,
since this is the only sort of thing we'll accept
as coming directly from Him.
But He talks to us constantly
and in His language—
one that we don't understand
and that we hate to learn:
the language of sacrifice
and faith
and of a prodigiously vast plan
to save us—us and the whole world.
He speaks to us
through the happenings in our life,
by habitually frustrating our petty human schemes,
systematically thwarting our attempts to escape Him
and forever scuttling our plans to learn
how to do without Him.
And, gradually, He makes us tractable,
helps us grow accustomed to His ways
and, someday,
when we're bedridden,
stunned by failure,
alone and unhappy
or overwhelmed
by our powerlessness,
He brings us around
to listening to His language
and respecting His will.

Then we start living.
    Christ is no longer a stranger for us.
        When confronted by outsiders
                or some mystery
                or suffering,
      we're like the Apostles after the Passion:
        we don't dare ask who it is
           since we know right well it's the Lord.[19]

I believe it takes a harrowing preparation
    to understand the Passion and the Redemption.

After they'd been freed from concentration camp,
      some of our friends said,
    "The soldiers' derision,
    the scourging of Jesus at the pillar,
    the crowning with thorns,
    the stripping of His garments
    and the crucifixion—
      we used to think of all these things
        as scenes from another age,
          a wild blur of color
            or holy pictures depicting Bible episodes;
      but back there, in irons, it all became present to us."
At some moment or other,
    each of them had a chance to meet Christ,
    each must've recognized himself in Him.
At some station along their own Way of the Cross,
    they realized the great love
      that'd suddenly caught up with them.
When their clothing was ripped from their back,

then, for the first time, they understood
      why Jesus'd let Himself be stripped of His garments.
They looked at Him, and He at them;
      both met and recognized each other.
When they were beaten and humiliated,
      perhaps they thought, for a minute, of Him
            whom they'd begun to resemble.
They saw why Jesus'd willed to be outraged and scourged,
      and they found strength
            in the unobtrusive, silent, everlasting love
                  that'd been waiting for them there for centuries.
When they collapsed from exhaustion on death marches,
      they knew they were re-enacting other falls
                  and walking in other footsteps.
Beyond time and space,
      Someone'd thought of them,
      Someone'd gone before them,
      Someone'd suffered agonies
            to be there with them
      so that,
            when everybody'd abandoned them
            and all the love of their dear ones
                  could no longer protect or follow them,
            they might still have a friend,
                        a comrade in chains,
                        a companion on the Cross,
            and might behold the purest, noblest
                        and most consoling image
                        of what they'd become.
They couldn't help hearing the Word made flesh
      once it had been uttered in their midst.

"But," we protest, "I've tried reading the Gospels.
    I *have* read them.
    In fact, I've gone through them a great many times.
They just didn't do anything for me.
    The words meant nothing;
    the stories were too familiar;
    the characters, so dull;
    and those obscure passages bored me.
I didn't find Christ there."

Of course not!
    But that's because we didn't read them the way we should.
        We read them like any other book—
            for the story,
            for the ideas;
        whereas reading the Gospels means
            listening to Christ,
            touching Him
            and coming in contact with Him
                through faith.

Even when He lived on earth,
    He made no particular impression
        on those who thought He was just another man.
One day, as a crowd milled around, jostling and elbowing Him,
    a woman drew near
        with faith in her heart and one thought in her mind:
            "If only I can touch the tassel of His cloak,
                I'll be healed!"[20]
        She did—and was healed.
Then Jesus stopped.

"Who touched Me?" He asked.

Dull-witted, as usual, the Apostles answered,
 "Master, how can You ask such a question
  when there are so many people
   pressing about You on every side?"

But He ignored them and insisted,
 "Someone touched Me.
  I can tell My healing power's been at work."

By this time, everybody realized something serious'd happened.

They held their breath and backed away,
 then blurted out:
  "I didn't do anything."
  "Don't look at me!"
  "I didn't even come near Him."

And the poor woman,
 trembling and alone in the circle they'd cleared,
admitted, "The one who touched You—it was I."

Now, everybody'd touched Him,
 everybody'd hustled Him;
  still, nobody'd been cured or transformed.

Only one had touched Him with faith;
 and a profound sense of well-being coursed through her:
  she was cured.

As for us, we all read the Gospels now and then.
 But if we approach them like an ordinary book,
  they'll produce no extraordinary effect on us.

We have to read them the way we'd have touched Christ—
  with the same reverence,

the same faith,
the same expectancy.

If someone eats the Eucharistic bread unwittingly—
say, a curious altar boy who tastes a host
without realizing it's consecrated—
he doesn't commit a sacrilege,
but he doesn't receive Communion either.
He eats it like plain bread;
and, for him, it is:
it doesn't bring him a particle of grace.
Well, that's how it is for the Gospels, too:
read them without faith,
and we read them without profit.

Every morning, before Communion, we repeat,
"Lord, I'm not worthy to have You come to me;
but only say the word, and my soul will be healed."
Each of us has, in his own home, this Book
which is full of healing words.
Let's test our faith on them,
as that woman in the Gospels tested hers on Christ.
The poor soul had just one chance,
one go at it.
How happy she'd have been,
how certain of being cured,
if she'd had Jesus there in front of her
for a whole hour,
for two,
for as long as she liked!

That privilege is ours to enjoy.
> How glad we should be,
> how confident,
> how irrepressibly fervid!
> There'll always be more to hear.
> And we can't be deaf forever;
> someday, we'll learn
>> to listen as we should,
>> to hear Him with faith,
>> to understand Him as we're cured.

What must we do to read the Gospels with faith?
It surely isn't enough to believe
> that everything written there actually happened once:
>> we owe that much respect to any book of profane history
>>> by a reputable author.
To read the Gospels with faith is to believe
> that everything in them is actually happening now,
> that they're a book of revelation,
>> a book of discovery,
> that, far more than a history, they're a prophecy.

They tell us who we are
>> and what we're doing.
They tell us how God lived among men.
> But God continues to live with us.
>> He's always the same,
>> and so are we.
What the Gospels relate is still going on today.
> They show us our life,
>>> how God loves us

and how we treat Him—
how we mistreat Him, too.
So we mustn't read them like ancient history,
a pious memoir,
a sentimental pilgrimage,
but like the revelation they are:
a revelation of God
and of ourselves.
We're announced, foreseen and prophesied in them,
and we've only to find the right place,
the words
that concern us
and are spoken directly to us.

When we go to Communion,
we don't receive Jesus living two thousand years ago
but Jesus living today.
So, too, when we read the Gospels,
we shouldn't listen to Christ
speaking to somebody else
two thousand years ago,
but listen to Him
as He speaks to us
now.
The Gospels are a book of communion:
Jesus dwells in the Eucharist;
but in the Gospels, He speaks.
In olden times, when people were sorely tried or perplexed,
they used to open the Gospels at random
and read the first verse their finger fell on.
Naturally, they didn't always find the right answer,

but they received the comfort they needed:
    they'd communicated with Jesus,
    they'd heard His voice,
    they'd been raised to His level.
"If only I can touch . . ."
"Power emanated from Him and healed everyone."[21]

The Gospels are a parable of the Church,
    just as the Old Testament was a parable of the New.
Every story of ours,
    our entire history,
  was prefigured in the Gospels,
    just as Christ's was in the first part of the Bible.
"Then, beginning with Moses and going through
               all the prophets,
He explained what referred to Him
            in the whole of Scripture."[22]
"All that's but a shadow of things to come."[23]

Abel, the just man who suffered persecution,
  was a type of another just man,
    who suffered persecution
      and met death in offering sacrifice.
Betrayed, sold and abandoned by his own brothers,
  Joseph was an image of someone else
    who was betrayed, sold and abandoned by His brothers
      while feeding them the bread earned on the Cross.
Merely a beginning, a preparation,
  Joseph and all the just and all the suffering
    only foretold the coming of the most just—
      who'd also suffer most.

As he carried the wood for his own immolation,
Abraham's beloved son, Isaac, foretokened
the just one,
the innocent one,
the only-begotten,
the Son
in whom the Father was well pleased.[24]
The desert rock that ran water when struck three times
represented Christ.
"Our fathers all passed through the sea
and all drank the same spiritual drink,
for they drank from a spiritual rock
which followed them,
and that rock was Christ.
Now, all these things happened as a type
and as examples to us."[25]
Going out to vanquish Goliath with slingshot and staff,
little David embodied all the weakness of God in the world.
He was like God,
who came down to us loving and openhanded.
Just as Goliath stood for demoniacal pride and violence,
so David personified Christ
armed with no quarterstaff but His Cross.
"All these things," Saint Paul repeats,
"happened to them as a symbol,
so that,
being written down,
they could instruct us,
who live in the final stage of the world."[26]

But the Gospels are a parable, too.

"Until now, I've spoken to you in parables,"
    said Jesus at the Last Supper.
"The time is coming when I'll no longer do so
    but will tell you about the Father plainly."[21]
Christ's whole life is an outline, a presage, a prophecy
    of what'll take place till the end of time.
He was born once
        because He'd keep being born ceaselessly;
He lived once
        solely because He'd live on and on;
He was ignored and rejected once
        because He'd always be.
    The circumstances surrounding His birth,
            life and death,
        and His contemporaries' inly attitude toward Him,
            constitute an appalling forecast of what
                His presence
                and our reaction
            will be forever and ever.

God's word will continue to be a revelation
    provided we admit that it concerns us
                        and unmasks us.
"Yes, the word of God is living
                and operative
                and keener than any two-edged
                    sword;
        it penetrates deep enough to divide soul and spirit,
                            joints and marrow,
        and disentangles the thoughts and designs of our hearts.
No one can hide from Him:

everything's naked and open to His sight."[28]
When God manifests Himself to us,
    we perceive simultaneously who He is
                     and who we are.
As soon as Saint Peter began to apprehend the Lord,
    he cried out,
        "Go away from me—I'm a sinner!"[29]
In revealing Himself to us,
    God must necessarily reveal us to ourselves.

The Gospels are a mirror[30]
    where each of us may see himself,
        not merely reflected,
        but exposed and denounced.
The trouble is
    we generally use it to look at the other fellow
    and turn away incensed that he can be so stupid,
                          so malicious,
                          so blind.
We react like King Clovis, who,
        on hearing the story of Christ's Passion,
        exclaimed, "Ah, if only I'd been there with my Franks!"
The poor man didn't realize
    he'd done the same thing a hundred times himself
        and was capable of worse yet;
he was convinced
    only others were wicked enough to commit
            such wrongs.
        The word of God hadn't unmasked him.
In his mind, the Gospels shed light on the past,
                    not the present.

The light'd shone, but his darkness hadn't
grasped it.[31]
He'd go on not knowing what he was doing[32]
as he killed and plundered,
oppressed the weak and trampled the conquered.
Knowing about God hadn't taught him a thing
about himself.

So, too, with Saint Peter.
When Christ predicted his betrayal,
Peter took the mirror that'd been handed him
and immediately saw in it the betrayal of others.
"Even if everyone else abandoned You," he protested,
"I wouldn't!"[33]
From that moment on, it was inevitable:
he'd betray Christ
because he had refused the light.

David, on the other hand, mended his ways
because he heeded a prophet.
In the mirror of God's word, he saw himself as a sinner.

Sensitive, loving and courageous,
he's the most appealing hero in the Old Testament.
Recall his exploits,
his friendship with Jonathan,
his encounters with neurasthenic King Saul,
who wanted to kill him
at the very moment David was trying
to soothe his lord with harp music.
Saul tracked him down ruthlessly,

but, when David had the king at his mercy,
he contented himself
with cutting off the hem of the royal robe,
and then his heart hammered with remorse
for what he'd done to his master.
On learning what'd happened, Saul wept and exclaimed,
"You're more just than I,
for you've done me good
and I've rewarded you with evil."³⁴

Well, even David sinned.
With alarming speed,
he fell into a most cowardly and odious crime.
Enamored of Bethsabee,
he called her husband, Urias, back from war,
deceived him,
made him drunk
and finally had him killed by base treachery.
Then he married Bethsabee,
and their son,
though conceived in adultery,
was born in lawful wedlock.
Thus they saved appearances and observed the proprieties.
Everything seemed in order.
The lie was consummated.
But there was a prophet in Israel—
Nathan, a man through whom God's word
became "a living thing,
active
and efficacious"
and stripped the hypocrite

of the good conscience he'd donned.
Nathan came to David and said,
"Two men lived in the same town.
One was rich; the other, poor.
The rich man had a great many flocks and herds,
whereas the poor one had only a little ewe lamb,
which he raised in his own house
along with his children,
sharing his food and drink with her
and nestling her to his bosom.
In a word, she was like a daughter to him.
One day, the rich man entertained a guest, but,
instead of slaughtering one of his own animals,
he stole the poor man's single ewe
and served her up to the visitor."
David wrathfully broke in,
"As truly as God's living,
the man who did that deserves to die!
For his crime and his cruelty,
I'll make him give the pauper, not one sheep, but four."
And Nathan said,
"That man is you!"
Then David saw himself for what he was—a sinner.
As soon as he stopped considering Nathan's parable
as a story
and accepted it
as a revelation and a prophecy,
he was shorn of his sincere yet canting indignation.
He knew what he'd done.
His eyes were opened and he confessed,
"I've sinned against God!"

So deeply had the light penetrated into him
  that he was forgiven immediately.
Nathan declared,
   "God has already blotted out your sin."[35]
  God's word is surely potent!

It'll be so for us, too,
  when we start reading it
     and constantly telling ourselves,
   "That man is I."
We're the innkeepers of Bethlehem
  who've no room for Him.
We're Herod
  and we deem this newborn king of the Jews
        a nuisance,
        a troublemaker,
    to be gotten rid of at any cost.
When we can finally admit that the verse
    "He came to His own"
    means us,
  the Gospels suddenly take on a whole new light.
We understand why He was received so coolly,
    why people refused to believe in Him,
    why He was so poor,
      so incredibly destitute.
We recognize the swaddling bands,
    the crib
    and the stable
      where we've lodged Him with animals.
We discover
  why His contemporaries were

so stubbornly opposed to Him,
so hardhearted.
We know, because we're the same.

His Passion and Death clear up, too.

The Passion starts all over again every day.
This year, other actors are playing the same roles—
millions and millions of indifferentists,
cowards
and yes-men;
those who gladly wash their hands of it,
who tolerate anything
as long as it's happening to the other fellow,
who don't want to take sides
"in these controversial matters,"
who don't do anything,
but without whom such things'd never be
done—
for the wickedness of the few breaks out
only when it can count on the
weakness of the many.
(How often have we sat, criminally unconcerned,
with injustice and tragedy being perpetrated
under our very eyes?)

Next come the millions of runaways:
people like Saint Peter
who, under pressure, deny they ever knew Christ.
Oh, they've heard many a sermon
and they've been moved:

it gave them such a nice holy feeling around the heart.
They were always there, marching in every procession.
They just loved miracles and traveled all over to see one;
    they've been to Lourdes, of course,
        and would even have toured Fatima.
But now,
    when everything's going wrong and prospects
        are dismal,
    when they're tasting blood and dragging a cross,
    when there are no more miracles
        and they themselves have to be the miracles—
            prodigies of faith,
                love
                and constancy—
they'll have nothing to do with Him,
they no longer recognize Him,
they act as if they'd never known Him.

Behind them come several thousand executioners.
    There's never a shortage of them,
        and they're always the same type:
    the tyrant cracking his whip,
    the savant with his biting comments,
    the petty official quoting his bylaws
    and the idler with his hankering for novelty.

Then there's the same Victim—
    with the same sorrowful face,
    infinitely patient
    and infinitely loving—
who doesn't say a word to us

but casts the same tender, questioning, reproachful glance
that tore open Peter's heart.
There are more victims than ever,
more good people suffering,
more innocents being persecuted:
twelve million orphans,
as many maimed by war,
millions of displaced persons,
millions of unusable senior citizens no one will hire
and millions of prisoners still in Communist prisons.
But why look so far afield?
In our own home or neighborhood
there are people who suffer and weep,
who are cold or hungry for something,
people who are sick or alone,
who are mourning, eating out
their heart.
There they are, looking at us and waiting. . . .
Who'll be Veronica
or Simon of Cyrene,
John,
Peter—
or Judas?

What a marvelous opportunity we have!
Jesus is here,
living among us,
suffering,
beginning His Passion all over again.
And we understand what's going on:
it's all been explained to us,

we've been given the key to this awful tragedy,
we've been told the actors' real names
and briefed on the true meaning of the drama.
All we have to do now is get on-stage and start acting.
The best thing is, we can choose our own role:
we can be
what we've always wanted to be for Christ;
we can see to it that,
in the huge mob of indifferentists and enemies,
He finds a few watchful servants,
a few attentive hearts,
a few loving faces,
a few signs of pity,
infinite compassion
and heartsick adoration.
We have enough faith to do it;
what we lack, unfortunately, is courage.

Christianity's a play we've been conning for a long time.
All the actors know it by heart.
We think we comprehend the Gospels.
"We've had enough of these courses," we moan,
"enough catechism lessons and sermons
and enough rehearsals.
We know our parts. We're ready. On with the play!"
So we strut out on to the stage.
But, once there,
we're blinded by the footlights,
distracted by the audience
and worried about our costume;
instead of playing our part,

we busy ourselves with trifles,
smoke a cigarette,
chat with bit players,
strike glamorous poses
or count the money in our wallet.
Suddenly, we hear a deafening roar.
The curtain falls,
the director runs onto the stage and shouts,
"What's the matter with you, anyway?
Why didn't you act?"
Taken aback, we mutter,
"We didn't know the play'd started.
We were waiting.
It wasn't the way we thought it'd be."

The fact is that the play did begin—and end,
but we weren't aware of it.
You see, it's never quite what we imagine it'll be.
Despite a thousand years of prophecy,
even the original actors missed their cues.
They kept thinking it should all be
different somehow.
Despite our Lord's warnings and intimations,
the very Apostles didn't know what was happening.

The uncomfortable feeling we have
that it's not going as it should
is the best proof that it's still going on in our day.
"Happy the servant whose master returns
and finds him up and ready!"[36]

"He who is of God hears His words"[37]—
　　living words
　　　　that are being spoken to us right now;
　　enlightening words
　　　　that tell us about God and ourselves;
　　dynamic words
　　　　that reveal us to ourselves
　　　　　　and sound the strongest call to conversion;
　　disturbing, discomfiting words
　　　　for those who grasp them,
　　　　　　　　expose their mind to them
　　　　　　　　and really try to live by them.
"He who is of God . . ."
　　When we love, we understand.
　　"Many refused to heed Him because their works
　　　　　　were evil."[38]
　　His sheep know His voice and follow Him.[39]

God's words are efficacious, too,
　　　　because they free us from our shamming
　　　　　　　　and our hypocrisy.
　　What time and energy we used to spend
　　　　　　putting on our mask
　　　　　　and fitting our costume!
　　He's finally ripped them off of us,
　　　　and now we're free—
　　　　　　　　free to do something else,
　　　　　　　　ready to perform another way:
　　　　　　　　His way.
"For just as rain and snow fall from heaven
　　and return only when they've soaked into the earth

and made it bloom,
giving new seed to plant
and bread to eat,
so will it be with the words I've spoken:
they'll not return to Me fruitless
but will produce whatever I wish
and prosper where I drop them.
Yes, you'll leave with joy in your hearts."[40]

His words are effective, lastly,
because we can give only what we've received
and describe only what we've seen.
"Come with me," the Samaritan woman urged the villagers
after talking with Jesus;
"come and see:
I've met someone who told me everything
I've ever done!"
While doing so,
He'd also revealed to her
who she was
and who He was.
After that, she couldn't do anything but talk about Him;
she had to share that revelation
and draw others to its source.
"Drink the water I give you,
and you'll never be thirsty again."[41]
We can draw others only to what we've experienced
and make them long only for the well
where we've quenched our thirst.

Our apostolate and all our activity

must be dictated by some word of God's
    loved, understood and correctly interpreted.
Consider the Samaritan woman.
    Immediately,
    heart and soul,
        she threw herself into—Catholic Action.
    And she did it right,
        for she convinced others to go discover for themselves
            the Prophet she'd found.
    Later, they gave her the only proof we can ever have
        that religious training's achieved its goal:
        "We believe," they said,
            "no longer because of what you've told us,
            but because we've heard Him ourselves
                and know He's the Saviour
                    of the world."[42]
They'd heard Him themselves,
    and, for them also, His word had become vital;
they'd listened closely
    and they, too, had been healed.

As for us,
    ours will be a living religion and an adult faith
        only when we can tell our catechists, retreat masters,
            parents and parish priests:
"I believe,
    no longer because of what you've said,
    but because I've heard Him for myself
        and I know He can save the world.
Until lately, all that meant nothing to me.
    I thought our Lord had redeemed us

two thousand years ago
and then withdrawn to heaven.
But now I've found out
that His saving power is still at work here below,
that a single word of His uplifts and cures us.
It's done that for me.
I can testify to it,
and I've a mission among my fellow men:
I believe that the world can be created,
saved
and restored
by a word from God."

THREE: *FORTUNATE ARE THE POOR*

The first requisite for understanding God's word is poverty.

But what does *poverty* mean?
    We mustn't oversimplify it,
        making it a merely material fact;
    that'd be as false
        as making it a purely spiritual aspiration.
The important thing isn't so much
        cutting down on our engine's horsepower,
        snipping the ruffles off our drapes
        or trimming a few yards from a cardinal's train.
Material poverty's an economic condition, not a virtue.
    If it sanctified us automatically,
        we'd be duty-bound to spread it
            rather than try to relieve it.
    Instead, we've been told, "Love one another,"[1]
        and not, as too frequently happens,
            "Impoverish one another."

Poverty doesn't necessarily lead to love,
    but true love always leads to poverty.
        In our own life, first of all. . . .
When only submitted to, and not chosen,
        poverty most often conceals burning cupidity.
The less wealth and pleasure we've tasted,

the more we desire them.
It's easier to despise what we have and know
than what we don't have
and what can delude us
because we aren't familiar with it.
There's a kind of poverty that turns people away from God.
That's why we're called to alleviate it
so as to prove God's love:
He needs us to manifest Himself to the poor
and turn their want into trust.
"Fortunate are the poor in spirit."[2]
That means:
Fortunate are those who are willing
to let themselves be censured by the word of God,
to re-examine their views,
to believe they haven't yet understood a thing,
to be taken by surprise,
to have their mind changed,
to see their convictions,
their principles,
their tidy systems
and everything they took for granted
swept out from under them,
and to face the fact, once for all,
that there's no such thing as a matter of course
and that God can ask anything.

Over the years, we've all grown a shell—
the concretion of intellectual, moral and emotional habits—
that admirably shuts us off from God.
It clings to us on all sides

just as we cling to it;
and the very thought of giving it up implies such a wrenching
that we adhere to God
only insofar as He doesn't require that,
only insofar as He doesn't dare demand that sacrifice.
"After all," we feel,
"He may as well say outright that He wants us to die!"
As a matter of fact, that's precisely what He does want.

The first degree of poverty God wishes from us
consists in renouncing our concept of poverty.
We habitually deceive ourselves in one of two ways.
"I'm not attached to anything," we maintain;
"therefore, I can keep everything.
I'm poor at heart."
All right, let's try parting with something this very minute—
just to see whether it hurts,
for every state of soul necessarily expresses itself
in action.
Or we declare: "I deprive myself of a lot of things
that my father had,
that my neighbor owns
or that my friend,
who says he's such a good Christian,
hasn't given up.
So I've got a perfect right to talk poverty to others."
No, we're merely preferred a spiritual possession
to a material one.
And that's worse.
We should hurry up and buy what we've sacrificed
and relinquish our right to preach to anyone.

The humiliation of being rich
           is a first step toward poverty,
    whereas pride in one's poverty
           is the most dangerous of luxuries.
"I thank You that I'm not like this publican"[8]
    can easily become
"I thank You that I'm not like this Pharisee."

How can we tell whether we're poor in spirit?
    There are a few tests we can apply.
        For instance, how do we react
           when the Lord cuts our moorings
              materially or spiritually?
                Do we sing the *Magnificat?*
    Or how about when He asks us to change,
        not the time of our daily prayers
           or the frequency of our confessions,
        but our whole way of seeing a problem
           which vitally concerns us?
That's where He wants to get us—
    not on the surface,
    not on the outside.

Unlike modesty or the gift of tears,
    poverty's not some little extra virtue—
           the frosting on the cake, you might say;
rather, it's the essential condition
    for being accessible to God
        and open to His influence.

"Fortunate are the poor in spirit:

the kingdom of heaven is for them"⁴—
not for the others, did you notice?
Poverty's the port of embarkation.
Only the poor can get out of the ego,
start on their way
and learn to listen to something
besides themselves,
because they're counting on someone else,
because they know they'd never manage alone.
The worst sin we can commit is to tell God,
"Let me be. I'll work this out by myself.
I've got everything I need, and I'm happy.
You did a good job of creation, but—well, that's enough.
I lack nothing."
We're happy, we say.
With or without God?
If our soul's perfectly placid,
we should watch out:
He's certainly not there.

We're poor when we're willing
not to be at peace,
but to be reproved,
tormented
and driven out of ourselves by the voice of God,
and to set forth on our journey to Him.
Abraham's the first of the poor,
the first to believe in God's soul-stripping word.
"Set out from here," God commanded.
"Leave your belongings, your country, your heritage,
your culture, your ways and your past."

And, though not young when God took possession of him,
Abraham left without knowing
where he was headed[5]—
a sure sign,
says Saint Gregory of Nyssa,[6]
that he was going the right way.
Abraham was poor at heart.
He accepted an utterly staggering invitation from God.

We're fettered by all sorts of riches
and all sorts of needs for more:
peace and comfort,
stability and security,
privacy and independence,
a yearning for refinement and the social graces,
a thirst for beauty, culture and intellectual joys.
Now, these things are good in themselves;
but if we're too attached to them,
we'll never be free to do God's work.
They were surely better bred in heaven than we on earth;
yet the Son left all that to live among us
till the end of time.

What's our ideal, our goal—
to become poorer and poorer
or richer and richer?
What direction are we working in?
How are we orienting our lives?

There's no one course
to guarantee we'll pass our exam on poverty;

no set answers, no sure-fire method.
Poverty that can be acquired
    because it's definite and ready-made
  is a contradiction in terms:
            an "acquisition" pure and simple,
            just one more possession.

We'll be poor when we can rejoice
    at seeing the branches cut from under us day after day.
Adam refused to let himself be dethroned from a tree,
        because he lacked the spirit of poverty.
And we—what tree is it we hold fast to?
            What limb do we jealously clutch?
            What domain do we block off and keep
                for ourselves?
    "That? Oh, no! There's no use asking.
        The rest, yes—all the other trees, the other fruit.
        But not this tree. It's mine.
        I do have to keep something for myself, you know."
    That's the whole point:
      God wants us to keep nothing
        so He can give us everything.

The real Poor Man is Christ.
    He kept nothing,
        clung to nothing—
            not even His sonship in a good family.
For They were a good family:
    They had a noble past and such lovely traditions:
        "No one knows the Son except the Father,
        and no one knows the Father except the Son."[1]

[69]

They lost Their social standing, however,
>   when They opened Their doors and let Themselves
>>>   be overrun
>>   by all of the Son's friends—
>   "those to whom He chose to reveal the Father."[8]
The nuptials of the Lamb?
>   Well, it wasn't a very good match.
He married beneath Himself;
in fact, He married—the earth:
>>   the Son lowered Himself
>>>>>   to the level of the whole earth
>>>>   and became "the true light
>>>>>   that enlightens every man
>>>>>>   who comes into the world."[9]
He didn't live according to His station, either.
>   "He abased Himself and,
>>>   though He was God by nature,
>   didn't hold tenaciously to His equality with God
>>   but emptied Himself
>>>   assumed the condition of a slave,
>>>   looked exactly like the man next door
>>>   and,
>>>>>   for all His neighbors could see,
>>>   was nobody special."[10]

Abraham,
>   as well as every call,
>>>   every exodus
>>>   and every exile of the Old Testament,
>   was but a prophecy.
There'd come a day when Someone'd do those things

completely,
totally—
Someone who,
though He had everything,
would surrender it all
to receive it all again from the hands of the Father.
"No one takes My life from Me,
but I lay it down Myself
so that I may take it up again.
That's why My Father loves Me."[11]

The first people who met Christ understood—
no, that's not right:
they couldn't have understood,
because God hadn't yet explained;
rather, they sensed, they perceived—
that they had to let God work in them.
They let Him do what He pleased,
trusting in Him
though they "didn't know where they were going
or where it'd all lead them."[12]
And then, later, they realized
that that was the only way God could act,
the only way they could be reached,
moved
and saved.
They also saw what God's like—
not at all what they'd imagined.
To quote Voltaire,
"God created men in His image,
and they've surely got even with Him for it."

[71]

Everyone has his own preconceived notion of God,
which nothing can change;
but that, too, we must give up—
that, before all else.

The first revelation of God came with the Beatitudes.
And the first beatitude is poverty—
that is,
the willingness to rise above all our earthly concepts,
all our fancies
and images.
The first revolutionary insight,
the first shocking disclosure,
was that God's poor.

The Jews ("those wicked Jews!") thought
our Lord was going to show them the God they
already knew.
(Are we quite certain we've outgrown that mentality?
How do we react to the unexpected?
Haven't we sometimes felt tricked
by the ever-changing face God keeps showing us?)
They'd done such a thorough job of figuring Him out,
and now it'd be so gratifying
to hear their views resoundingly confirmed,
to feel still surer than before,
still more snugly ensconced,
still quicker with answers
for those who'd question their authority:
"God's mighty and awesome and rich,"
"Be good,

and He'll reward you with health, wealth
and sons,
make you prosperous
and fill your storerooms,"
"This misfortune's befallen you due to some sin,"
"I've just inherited a lot of money.
You know how it is:
God takes care of the good,"
and so on, and so on.

We must note
how drastically they'd narrowed the perspectives
of the Old Testament
to arrive at this idea of God,
for the Bible's filled with the exodus and the exile,
with Abraham and Joseph
and Moses and Job,
all the prophets
and a litany of "good people"
who got a thorough drubbing.
But in Jesus' day
the Jews were firmly convinced that, now especially,
God would always be the Dependable Distributor
who crowned their system so nicely.
That's the notion they wanted Christ to corroborate
once and for all.
"Sing us the old theme we've developed so well
over the centuries."
They wished nothing more from Him.

But Christ sat on the mountainside and declared,

"Fortunate are the poor . . ."[13]
Thunderstruck, His hearers decided
He wouldn't get away with that sort of thing.
"A joke's a joke, but He's carrying it too far.
We have to shelter the children from such nonsense!
What's this world coming to, anyway?
And how about our families, our rights,
our ancestors and our father Abraham?"
(They were forgetting
that He'd pauperized their father Abraham
in one sentence.)

Too bad, but even the Apostles'd have a lot of trouble
relinquishing this belief
and seeing their theology overturned.
Came the Ascension—
the last act, the final scene
of His visible life among them—
and what did they say?
"When are we going to be invested?"[14]
All they could envision was
twelve thrones,
twelve superb spiritual installations,
twelve grateful heavenly rewards,
twelve official seats
and twelve palm branches.

But Christ stayed there
and kept describing the attributes of God:
"Fortunate are the poor. . . .
Happy are those who weep"[15]—

which means:

Happy those who can't be happy by themselves,

who aren't self-sufficient,

who aren't content to save

their own souls.

As for Bethsaida and Corozain and Jerusalem,

Jesus wept over them.[16]

We mustn't understand "Happy are they who whimper,"

for joy, too, is a characteristic of God:

"Father, may they taste the fulness of My joy!"[17]

Still, there's a godly sorrow, mentioned by Saint Paul,[18]

which consists in not tolerating injustice.

Now, the injustice is this:

that souls are lost through our fault.

If we're not overwhelmed,

not completely floored by our helplessness

when we consider all the wrong,

all the bitterness

and all the misery in the world,

then we're not living according to this beatitude

and not responding the way God does.

Fortunate are those who can't help being roused

by their neighbor's misfortune—

his sins,

his anguish,

his ignorance,

his blindness

and his crushing failures.

Happy those who suffer

because they can't lighten the sufferings of others.

There's peace in store for those who are obsessed

        by the desire to change the world
           and help save it.

"Lucky are the meek"[19]—
   not the jellyfish,
   but the tenacious and the patient,
      those who can take it and stand adversity
         without giving up,
      those who can bend
        and not vent their anger on everyone around,
      those who can wait,
      those who, in darkness, can believe
         what they saw in the light.
A meek man's the contrary of a rebel.
   When they encounter hardship,
     rebels quit,
     but meek men persevere.
  People with a cozy, set philosophy,
        though they, too, are the opposite of rebels,
    resemble them in one respect:
        they quit also—
          but for different reasons:
    they use everything to further their interests,
    whereas rebels tend to destroy what doesn't
        benefit them.
Midway between the two stand the meek,
  who realize they mustn't let go at any cost
         but rely on God,
           count on Him,
           leave everything to Him
           and then trust.

"There'll be satisfaction for those
                    who hunger and thirst for justice" [20]—
    for that justice which,
            in Biblical terminology,
                is practically synonymous with *truth*.
        Rightness, we could call it.
More than any other,
    this hunger and thirst'll completely empty us of ourselves.
            "Go forth. . . . Depart from here."
    We'll perpetually have to be leaving something behind:
                            our milieu,
                            our habits,
                            everything.
    We'll have to do things we've never done before,
        and it'll hurt.
    We'll have nowhere to rest our head from now on, [21]
            no more approbation to help us along,
            not a point on which to feel encouraged,
                            sustained
                            and carried
                            forward
                by a reassuring and conniving past.
When we let ourselves be censured by the word of God,
    we can expect to be sharply upbraided.
There's not an aunt who won't voice her opinion—
            unfavorable, of course.
        "Every day they taunt me:
            'Where's that God of yours?'" [22]
For He doesn't generally give us
                a corner of the Promised Land
        to conjure up and silence our critics with.

All Abraham got out of it, for instance, was his grave.

"Happy are the merciful,"[23]
    those who know how to forgive—
which is another way of saying:
        Happy are they who can take the first step.
There's nothing more revolutionary than someone who,
        right in the middle of a feud,
    suddenly turns around and forgives.
We're all such monkeys by nature!
    What someone does to us
            we do to him—
                either the same thing
                or the equivalent.
    And there's no way out,
        since we've drawn an infernal circle about ourselves
            and can only pace around it,
                calmly and coldly,
                    forever.
    Indeed, how can we get anywhere,
        seeing that we've agreed to disagree
            once and for always?

There's only one solution,
    and that's for us to conceive the stupendous idea
        of starting to love someone who doesn't love us.
Then we'll be doing something new.
    When we render blow for blow,
        we're just imitating the other fellow;
    whereas if we don't strike back
        but rather forgive

and show signs of love,
and if we say,
"Look, now; we can't go on like this.
It's all too petty, too stupid.
Let's make up: there's so much more to life!"—
if we do that,
we produce something absolutely unprecedented
on earth,
we dynamite the prison
which discord slowly but steadily built about us.
As it is now,
if we take someone's cloak,
we can be sure he'll refuse us his tunic.[24]
That's how we expect him to act,
and we're not the least bit surprised.
But suppose he *did* give us his tunic,
we'd be stunned.
Who ever heard of such a thing!
Recalling the Gospel text
"No one's ever done the like before,"
we'd say, "This man thinks for himself"
and we, too, might start reconsidering
the whole problem.

"Happy are the merciful"—
those who manage to shake off the indolence
that makes us follow suit all through life.
Happy are those who break through the vicious circle
of our tiresome squabbles,
our rancor
and our grudges.

"You can't love only such as love you!
Don't even pagans do that?"[25]
We must be different—
original, as our heavenly Father is;
merciful
and, therefore, creative.
God didn't let sin wall Him up in His heaven;
He didn't conceal Himself behind a thunderhead,
sulking because man was.
When Adam hid among the trees,
God didn't withdraw but took the first step,
as He always does:
"Where are you, Adam?[26]
Come on, old man, let's start all over!"
The only dealings that strike us as being sensible
are invariably the ones that enslave us most:
lending to people who'll repay us in full,
smiling at those who smile at us.
But smiling at someone who'll spit in our face
and helping a man who'll turn his back on us—
those are free, creative acts.

"Blessings on the peacemakers,"[27]
those who won't tolerate cold wars and endless wrangling.
Blessings on those who won't shrug their shoulders and whine,
"Nothing can be done."
Let's make no mistake about it:
peace has nothing to do with tranquility;
there's often no more exhausting,
no more disturbing, task
than establishing peace between two people.

True peace, of course.
    "May the Lord's peace always be with you!"
He promised, "I give you *My* peace,"
    reminding us that He gives it
        "not as the world does."[28]
To receive it, we have to be perfectly guileless;
    and, as in any form of life,
        that presupposes total disarmament
                and prior death,
    for God gives His peace only to those
     who surrender to Him unconditionally.

"Fortunate are they who suffer persecution."[29]
    They're the ones
        whom God's already begun to dislodge from their nest,
    who long to be liberated
    and whom He loves so much
        that He can't wait for them any longer.
      He's in such a hurry to have them near Him,
           freed from themselves,
      that He'd rather get to work personally
        and start shaking them loose right away.
      (Our eagerness to throw ourselves into God's arms
          is usually so well controlled
      that we wouldn't get there very fast
        unless He snatched us up Himself.)
"Rejoice and exult"—
      Saint Luke reads "Leap for joy"[30]—
    "because your reward in heaven is great."[31]
Now, we know that whenever God says "reward,"
    He's not dickering about something in the future.

He pays ahead of time—here and now.
"You're being persecuted," He says,
                "insulted, belittled and calumniated?
Well, be glad:
        it's because they're thinking of you in heaven.
                God desired you so vehemently
                        that He wanted
                                and had to have you at once.
        That's how past generations treated the prophets."[32]
And that's how man's always treated God.
        For the Beatitudes are theological,
                and, in them, Jesus tells us what God's like:
                        poor and humble,
                        meek and merciful,
                        peacemaking and persecuted.

The Beatitudes let us enter into God's own life.
        He can communicate Himself only to the poor
                since they're the only ones
                        He has anything in common with.
God is a giver:
        the Father's sole joy lies in giving;
        the Son's, in receiving and giving back.
                "Father, all that's Yours is Mine,
                        and all that's Mine is Yours."[33]
The poor share in this exchange,
                        in this divine flow of life;
        but the rich obstruct it.
        That seems to explain Christ's answer
                        to the disciples of John the Baptist
                as He justified His mission by answering,

"The poor have the Gospel preached to them."[34]
The poor—
in other words, all those who are sufficiently detached,
disposable
and free
to enter into the tremendous divine joy
of a gift received and passed on.
Here's proof that God's come and manifested Himself:
He fulfills the expectation of the poor.[35]

A first confrontation with the living God,
the Beatitudes throw light on Him
and on us.
At one and the same time,
we begin to see what He is
and how different we are.
The Gospels act as a developer
and produce on a sensitized plate
the image that was invisible to us before.
Through them, God manifests Himself to us
more and more clearly,
till He finally shows us a Face
which He wants us to reproduce.
He points out the road He Himself has chosen
and, like a friend, urges us to walk it with Him.
What's our answer been?
How did those people respond
who sat around Him there on the mountainside?
What would we have done?

When God offers us His blessedness,

He first provokes two terribly violent reactions in us:
on the one hand,
indignation, refusal, anger and panic;
and on the other,
desire and an attraction filled with dread.

Jesus talked absolutes,
compelled everyone to make a crucial, clear-cut choice.
Suddenly, with nowhere to hide
and nothing to latch on to,
they reeled,
dizzy from the heights where He'd transported them.
Then some recoiled in hatred and terror,
repudiated Him from the start
to be proof against Him to the end,
and didn't stop running
till they'd safely gone to ground.
"There's a limit," they stormed.
"This is outrageous.
What right's He got to ask so much?"
So, from then on, they avoided meeting Him,
hearing Him speak
and thinking of Him.
It's always been very easy to escape from God.
He forces no one
but waits and calls—with infinite patience,
powerless against those
who refuse to look into His eyes
and listen to His voice
but prudently pretend they don't recognize Him.
"And you—are you going to leave Me, too?"[86]

But others,

      just as frightened and overwhelmed and dazed,

  kept listening.

And the more He spoke,

    the more they sensed, the more they realized

      that they'd always wanted

        someone who'd make these unheard-of

          demands;

      that they'd always waited,

          so they could believe in Him,

        for someone who'd dare exact so much

          from them;

      and that only a rigorous exigency like this

        could match their vast desires.

The whole experience was like a dew

    that instantly quickened the deepest part of them.

They understood

    that this alone could be true religion

    and that only He who'd have them renounce so much

      could also help them do without.

The greatest sacrifice, they saw,

          afforded the greatest liberation,

    since He'd have to supply them with everything

          He'd stripped them of.

Such total love presupposed total care on His part:

    they merely had to throw themselves on His mercy,

      merely entrust to Him the whole adventure

        on which He'd so boldly launched them.

          From now on, it was His business!

And what a joy,

    for each one saw his youthful dream coming true,

as he remembered how he'd once longed
to do precisely this:
to surrender,
love
and find fulfillment so.

"God heaps up good things for the hungry"[37]—
those who are willing and glad to be poor,
despoiled,
dispossessed,
uprooted.
He'd whispered the Beatitudes in Mary's heart
before promulgating them to the crowd;
and she,
perfectly attuned and thoroughly thrilled,
had answered with her *Magnificat*,
the triumphal hymn of the Beatitudes.
He'd thwarted all of her plans
and she rejoiced
because He'd looked upon the poverty of
His handmaid.
When we empty ourselves,
commit our lives to Him
and, like the poor, look to Him for everything,
we make room for Him to work in us.
He topples the mighty from their thrones
and banishes the proud far from His presence,
but fills the hungry with good things
and draws to His side the lowly,
those who are available
and ready

for anything,
like Abraham "and his race forever."
And for such as these, He performs wonders.[38]

FOUR: *GOD IS LOVE*

"We've come to know love and believe in it,"[1]
    writes Saint John.
"Naturally," we protest.
   "How could anyone not believe in love
      once he's known it?
   How fail to recognize it
      once it's been revealed to him?
   Under those conditions,
    who wouldn't love it
           and cling to it fervently
           and gladly share in all its designs
                   wishes
                   and concerns?"

Are we so sure of that?
   How do we react to, say, the parable
         about the workers of the eleventh hour?
   Does the master's astounding justice
      elate us, move us and set us at ease?
  And what about the story of the prodigal son?
   Haven't we ever caught ourselves saying,
     "He didn't come back till he got good and hungry,
     Wasn't that a fine thing, though!
     And, all the while, the poor elder brother
        sweated away

[91]

fattening the calf they'd roast for that rake
as soon as he deigned to remember
he had a family.
Then, there was the best robe, the banquet,
the music and the dancing. . . ."
Haven't we ever felt
that the father overdid it somewhat?
At any rate, the elder son,
a serious young man,
a hard worker
and a good Christian,
didn't like it one bit.
He saw love—and grew indignant.

In one of his plays,
Jean Anouilh describes the last judgment as he sees it.
The good are densely clustered at the gate of heaven,
eager to march in,
sure of their reserved seats,
keyed up and bursting with impatience.
All at once, a rumor starts spreading:
"It seems He's going to forgive those others, too!"
For a minute, everyone's dumfounded.
They look at one another in disbelief,
gasping and sputtering,
"After all the trouble I went through!"
"If only I'd known this . . ."
"I just can't get over it!"
Exasperated, they work themselves into a fury
and start cursing God;
and at that very instant they're damned.

That was the final judgment, you see.
    They judged themselves,
        excommunicated themselves.
Love appeared,
    and they refused to acknowledge it.
        "We don't know this man."[2]
        "We don't approve of a heaven
            that's open to every Tom, Dick and Harry."
        "We spurn this God who lets everyone off."
        "We can't love a God who loves so foolishly."
And because they didn't love Love,
        they didn't recognize Him.

Yet love does things like that,
    and we have to expect such surprises from God.
He wants us to learn to identify **Him**
    by the way He loves.

Do we love Love?
Do we like the way He loves?
Do we believe that He alone knows how to love,
    that He alone can teach us to love?

Many people imagine that what holds them back from God
    is their fondness for this world,
        their affection for each other
        and all the warmth of life.
They talk as if these things were an obstacle.
    "We're too human to be truly religious," they lament,
        "too sensitive, too loving,
           too taken up with everything around us,

too earthly, too burdened with care;
and there are too many things—
children and home, garden and career—
that we couldn't love any more."
But that's just it:
if we'd known Jesus,
we'd have found in Him
such a living source of love,
such a fresh interest in the world around Him,
such a genuine and unprecedented burst of
tenderness
that we'd have learned this lesson:
He alone knows how to love,
love well
and love enough,
and we, on the contrary, don't know how
and are pitiably lacking
in love.

Jesus observed everything,
was entranced by trifles
and glorified the Father at every turn.
How He loved nature!
He looked so much more intently than we
at the trees,
the meadows
and the fields "already white for the harvest"*—
all familiar sights
for which perhaps we've never thanked God.
He was born in a cave,
died on a hill

and spent the most excruciatingly human night
of His life
in an orchard.
The Gospels are full of the great outdoors
and the open road.
And how well Christ knew
the weather portents in the sky,
the thoughts of men on earth,
the beauty of the flowers of the field
and the habits of the birds of the air!
When He'd had enough of men
and their petty bickering,
their grievances
and their selfish requests,
their deliberate thick-
headedness
and their hard hearts,
He'd go off in a boat
with His small circle of faithful friends
and breathe in the brisk sea breeze.
"That day, Jesus went out of the house
and sat by the water's edge."⁴

Have we ever stopped to think,
when seeking a bit of solitude or a whiff of clean air
before starting the day,
that He once did the same thing,
that He experienced the same needs
and the same simple pleasures?
The only difference is that He appreciated them
a hundred times more,

a hundred times better than we do.
He looked through everything
and discovered the divine reality
on which it'd been patterned.
He really saw the world and loved it.
For Him, it was shot through with symbols
("sacraments," we'd say now),
rich with meaning,
filled with the Spirit.
All of it signified something beyond.

For example, at the sight of water,
whether in a lake or in a fountain,
He'd muse: "Water's a good thing."
"Give Me some water," He asked the Samaritan woman
but added,
"If only you knew the water I can give you—
real water,
living water,
water that'll quench your thirst forever."[5]
His eyes wandered over the vineyards—
a beautiful picture, too,
as were the vine-dressers trimming them.
"My Father's the vine-dresser."[6]
He noted bread was tasty, nourishing and beneficial
and declared,
"I'm the true bread that sustains life."[7]
He watched mothers and fathers with wonder
and concluded,
"It's amazing that,
evil as you are,

you can be so good to your children.
Well, from that try to fathom the goodness of Him
who's truly a father,
every inch a father,
the Father. . . .[8]
No one knows the Father
except the Son
and those the Son chooses to reveal Him to."[9]
After walking the length and breadth of Palestine,
He stated,
"I love your roads, your footpaths and your lanes,
and I've used them so often!
Still, where do they lead?
I'm the way. . . .[10]
I've passed by so many of your homes and stopped in;
I've found so many of your doors inviting.
But I'm the door,[11]
and, through Me,
you'll enter into the house of My Father,
who's waiting for you."
Thus, He took all these familiar earthly things,
which we most certainly should love,
and taught us
what divine perfection they mirrored
and for whose glory they'd been created.

We all remember the scene in which Jesus,
taking a little child
and setting him in the midst of the Twelve,
warned them they'd have to become like him.
But how many recall the telling detail Saint Mark relates?

The poor tot was no doubt scared and ready to cry
    when he saw all those grownups staring at him,
        so Jesus "took him into His arms."[12]
There was Christ,
        ready to expound to the Apostles
            a key point in His message;
    but that didn't stop Him from turning His attention,
            first of all,
        to this openmouthed child.
He consoled and reassured him,
        made him feel at home,
    and only after that continued with His teaching.

Jesus is more human (in the true sense of the word),
    more loving,
        more tenderhearted
            than the most sensitive of us.
One day, He sat in the Temple with His followers
    observing the people
        as they walked by
            and dropped coins into the treasury.
The curious Apostles'd look,
                    guess at the amount put in
                    and then comment on it.
    "That's So-and-So,
        and that's that Other Fellow. . . ."
Our Lord suddenly asked,
    "Who do you think gave most?"
Naturally, they tried to remember
        whose money'd made the loudest clank,
    and Jesus had to start explaining everything,

educating them all over again.
"Didn't you notice that woman back there?
No, you didn't read her face;
you didn't see that she put in
everything she had to her name.
In fact, I tell you . . ."[13]
And the Apostles found out
that they hadn't really seen anything,
that they were blind, dull and dense
even in their curiosity.
Only our Lord had loved that woman and,
because He had,
He'd seen and understood and guessed.
He always looked with sympathy
on everyone's trials and sufferings,
on his most secret afflictions
and most shameful grief.

To the least promising of men
He showed such love,
such unwonted and compelling trust,
that they'd become dazzling founts of generosity and faith.
Zacchaeus the parvenu,
the short, rich man everybody hated,
the publican who'd made an ivory tower
of his ill-gained wealth—
this Zacchaeus was freed for good and all
by a visit from Christ.
All it took was a glance and a cheerful greeting:
"Zacchaeus, hurry down!
I'm eating at your house today."

Zacchaeus welcomed Him joyfully and vowed,
    "Listen, Lord, I'll give . . ."
People expected nothing good from Zacchaeus,
    and so he expected nothing good from them.
And all at once here was Somebody
      who loved him,
        who enjoyed sitting at table with him
          and showed confidence in him.
Feelings that seemed forever dried up
      began to flood his being,
        buoy him up,
        transport
        and convert him.
Everyone else'd pushed him still deeper into his sterility;
everyone else'd decided to put up with him as he was:
      hopelessly evil and avaricious.
But Jesus'd hoped in him for all time.[14]

So it is in each of our families:
    there's almost always a black sheep
        whom we've judged incapable of good
           and coldly given up—
    usually a grandaunt or a distant cousin,
    but sometimes one of our children, our husband or wife.
      "I've tried every way I know.
      There's nothing that can be done.
      She's incorrigible.
      Well, I'm through!
      I'd be wasting my time
        trying to make her understand anything."
Here's a boy who, it seems, won't amount to much.

Our answer?

"Now we know what you think of us, young man!"
This girl looks like a little saint right now.

Our attitude?

"Just wait. She showed her true colors last winter."
We've an ungrateful, shifty, grasping, hypocritical brother
            who's never done anything but sponge on us.

Our verdict?

"I can't let him keep taking advantage of me.
For his own good, I wash my hands of him!"
Jesus, instead,
        would've paused in front of these people,
            looked at them with so much faith,
            and loved them with such disarming
                                simplicity,
                        such unaccustomed
                            tenderness
                        and infectious joy
that He'd have brought forth from their callous hearts
        inexpressible bursts of gratitude, wonder and rapture.

Our Lord expected the utmost from everyone.
Behind men's grumpiest poses
            and most puzzling defense mechanisms—
                respectability and seriousness,
                arrogance, dignified airs or coarseness,
                silence or cursing—
He could see a child
    who hadn't been loved enough
    and who'd stopped developing
        because someone'd ceased believing in him.

Appearances never fooled Him;
   He knew that people try to look wicked
                              as well as good,
                and that both kinds are equally piteous.
We've become so evil
   because no one's loved us
                or discovered the real *us*,
   because no one's inspired us
                or wanted us to be better.
     Inside of every human being
          God exists and waits to be detected
             so that He may thrive.

Loving people means summoning them forth
               with the loudest and most insistent of calls;
it means stirring up in them
   a mute and hidden being
          who can't help leaping at the sound of our voice[15]—
   a being so new
                that even those who carried him
                didn't know him,
        and yet so authentic
                that they can't fail to recognize him
                once they discover him.
All love includes fatherhood and motherhood.
   To love someone is to bid him to live,
                invite him to grow.
Since people don't have the courage to mature
       unless someone has faith in them,
   we have to reach those we meet
          at the level where they stopped developing,

where they were given up as hopeless,
and so withdrew into
themselves
and began to secrete
a protective shell
because they thought they were alone
and no one cared.
They have to feel they're loved very deeply
and very boldly
before they dare appear humble and kind,
affectionate, sincere
and vulnerable.
So many snarl
or stay aloof
or try desperately to be repulsive. . . .
How thirsty they must've been
to become so hard!
How they must've suffered
to become so bad!
And how we have to console them for all those wrongs!

Jesus knew how to go about it.
Our ranting and raving didn't frighten Him.
He understood what evil gripped us
and realized a single loving look would free us.
The man who was possessed—
and which of us isn't?—
shrieked,
"Let me be! Don't torture me, Jesus!
At last, I've found a stone to rest my head.
I've suffered too much,

and I don't want to go through that again.
If I started believing and hoping and loving now,
I'd have to risk the doubt,
the waiting
and all that pain
once more.
No, I just don't want Your love;
I don't want Your life.
Don't come any closer!"
That was despair.
But love is stronger than despair,
and so Jesus commanded the unclean spirit,
"Get out of this man."[16]

Unlike us,
our Lord didn't confuse the sinner and his sin,
the wicked and their wickedness.
He wouldn't identify people with what was known
about them
(which is the most discreet, speedy and
common way we have
of killing our neighbor,
of making it impossible for him to go on living).
Christ went much deeper than that.
Beyond the shouting,
He saw the men who hadn't yet begun to shout,
the children who hadn't begun to suffer;
He saw their boundless desire to love and be loved—
till they withdrew and bolted their hearts fast
because there was no one near to answer.
Well, He answered.

He picked up the thread of their life
    at the exact spot where everyone else'd dropped it;
He revived their love
    at the stage where everybody'd let it die;
He discovered in each one that bower of innocence
        where God takes His delight,
           where He can communicate Himself to man,
              permeate his being,
              speak to him
              and give Himself entirely.

That's why He couldn't put up with
        our reservations about this and that,
        our disparaging remarks
        and our hasty judgments.
For instance, He defended Mary Magdalene
        against everybody:
    against Judas,
        who'd accused her of throwing away money;
    against Martha,
        who'd called her lazy;
    and against Simon,
        who'd said nothing but had his own
           opinion of her.
This Simon, a Pharisee, had invited Jesus to dinner
    and, when he saw Mary at the Lord's feet,
        he thought disgustedly:
           "If this man were a prophet,
              He'd surely know who's touching Him;
              He'd know she's a sinner."
Jesus immediately turned to him.

"Simon, may I say something?"

"Speak, Master, by all means."

"A certain man had two debtors,

one of whom owed him five hundred gold pieces
and the other, fifty.

Since they couldn't possibly pay their debt,

he let them both go scot-free.

Now, tell Me, which one'd love him more?"

Simon, who was a usurer, replied,

"The one who received the greater favor, I'd say."

"Yes, Simon, you're right.

In this, you've judged correctly. . . .

But when I entered your home,

you didn't give Me any water for My feet,

whereas she,

from the moment she entered,

hasn't stopped bathing them with her tears
and wiping them with her hair;

you didn't kiss Me,

whereas she . . ."[17]

From that we learn how tender Jesus was,

sensible to any token of affection
and vulnerable to all unkindness.

And we,

have we ever thought of receiving Him

otherwise than Simon did?

And don't we,

who consider ourselves so thoughtful,

deserve the same reproach:

"You didn't kiss Me"?

Everybody in town deemed Simon a saint, a "just man,"
                    and Mary Magdalene
                              a lewd woman.
Jesus alone sees us as we really are.
While some of Newman's illustrious friends lay in state
          and he watched mourners file past
                    who thought they'd known them,
     he mused on the true face
               these dead also must've preserved
                         from childhood days—
          a face unknown to all but the Lord
                              and perhaps a few intimates
                                   who'd sincerely loved
                                        them.

There's something sonly in each human being;
          but how well he hides it,
          and how unskillful we are at finding it!
"In the most heartless miser," wrote Claudel,
     "deep within the prostitute and the filthiest drunkard,
          there's an immortal soul
               which is holily busy breathing
               and which,
                    barred from daylight,
               makes nocturnal adoration."
Conrad observed that in the fiercest pirate
     there's a port of guilelessness
          accessible only to similar guilelessness.
We'll never establish real contact with anyone
     until we stop arguing and chaffering

               and give proof of our uprightness,
                        loyalty
                        and sincerity;
but once we succeed,
    we can expect complete fidelity.

"We've come to know love and believe in it."
Simon the Pharisee didn't believe in it
    for the simple reason that he didn't want to.
We open our door only to someone who knocks;
    we find only what we're looking for.
Like the rest of the Pharisees, Simon wanted
        only one thing:
        recognition of his worth,
        just recompense for his meritorious deeds.
Since he'd earned heaven on his own,
    he felt he didn't need the "gift of God"
        which meant life for Mary Magdalene.
This sudden liberality, this business of forgetting debts
        didn't appeal to him at all:
    for some twenty, thirty or forty years now,
        he'd carefully seen to it
            that he owed nothing to anyone.
And he was irritated, too, by the way Christ had
    of changing people altogether with one look,
        creating in them a new personality
        according to His own will.
Simon was quite satisfied with himself the way he was
        and didn't mind telling you how,
        from childhood up,
    he'd worked hard at all sorts of tedious virtues

to become what he was now:
a respectable man.
But that Mary Magdalene—
no one'd ever accuse her of being virtuous
or of troubling herself about it.
"Simon, there's something I want to tell you.
Those who need little forgiveness feel little love."[18]
But Simon couldn't understand.
These words made no impression on him
because his mind had grown full and dull;
he didn't grasp their meaning
because he lacked that sixth sense—
the spirit of poverty, humility and love.

"My sheep hear My voice and know Me."[19]
They recognize His call,
without His having to explain or justify anything,
because He moves them deeply
and His constraining love requires
an immediate answer:
complete and humble faith.
"He who is of God hears His words."[20]
He carries nothing with him
but raises his open hands to receive God's gift,
and he already prefers the son or the daughter
God will love in him
to the barren, solitary being he dragged along
because he had nothing better to offer.
Since he's free from pride and pretense,
he's aware of the things of God
and responsive to Him.

Our senses help us identify objects.
Fragrances, sounds and tactile impressions
tell us about our surroundings.
When we're exposed to inclement weather
or overtax our strength,
we soon know it:
we receive danger signals within
and realize we shouldn't ignore them.
So, too, there are spiritual senses
that accurately disclose the true nature of men,
objects
and events.
A place where many people have worshiped
is instinct with prayer
and conducive to it.
Anyone with keen spiritual senses wakens to this feeling
and reacts accordingly.
A beautiful ceremony,
a Mass celebrated in an atmosphere of recollection,
a good prayer, Communion or confession
uplifts and renews us.
And there's no denying
that a spiritual person,
a genuinely pious one,
a saint,
has a secret power
that draws all who think the way he does.
We can even check our spiritual condition by asking ourselves
how we've been affected by the holiest people we've met:
Have we been attracted to them,
influenced by them,

made humbler and more fervent?
Unfortunately, we'll often discover
we've been rubbing elbows with them for years
without suspecting how saintly they are.

To all appearances, Jesus was like everyone else.
People who saw only externals
found nothing that set Him apart from them.
After all, He dressed the way they did. . . .
And the fact is that He came and went
and walked and talked and slept
exactly like the rest of them.
But the heedless crowd didn't notice this
one big difference:
He never sinned.
Only those with a glimmer of living faith,
a spark of spiritual life,
perceived that
and were moved and drawn to Him,
though they often couldn't tell why.
When He came near,
the deepest and most vital parts of their being
began to stir
and prodigious floods of joy and love,
of infinite and sweet
bewilderment,
welled up from their innermost heart.

All Christ's apparitions after He rose from the dead
were meant only for this:
to help us discern His overwhelming presence

beyond any and every outward appearance.
"Mary Magdalene thought it was the gardener.
Then He called to her, 'Mary!' "[21]
"On the shore, they saw a stranger looking at them. . . ."[22]
Each time, they seize this unprovable certitude more eagerly
and identify Him sooner.
They learn to recognize Him
because of an impression He creates—
an impression He alone can produce in us.
As the disciples from Emmaus put it,
"Didn't our heart just burn within us
while He was explaining the Scriptures?"[23]

How did they know it was He that time?
"They recognized Him in the breaking of the bread."[24]
That's all:
a bit of food
unexpectedly divided and shared
in some inn or other
where He'd gone for friendship's sake.
"Stay with us. It's getting late."[25]
That's all:
an invitation,
a "yes"
and a meal together.
There's how Christ has chosen to reach us.
There's the sort of proof,
the sort of grounds,
He gives us
to decide whether we'll be for Him or against Him.

"But," some wonder, "why that way?
Why not use force instead,
                    prestige and might and splendor—
        yes, even violence and something cataclysmic?
It'd be more dazzling and, therefore, more charitable:
        at least, everybody'd understand,
                    everybody'd comply."

Nobody'd understand.
    They'd all listen through selfishness
                    and comply through fear,
            when God wants nothing but love.
The only faithful revelation of the Father's love
        was the silent, palpable, defenseless presence of the Son.
On the Cross, He was bidden to manifest Himself
        and He answered—by staying right there.
That's how much He loved us
            (for loving means placing one's trust in somebody
                    forever):
        He loved us to the point of hoping
            that we'd love Him like that,
                    love Him up there on the Cross,
        and that we'd always be able to see Him
            in all the poor and all the outcasts,
                    the executed and the pursued,
                    the dying,
                    those who've wasted their lives,
                    the lonely, the weak and the oppressed.
Love, simplicity, lowliness,
        pain, compassion, poverty and death—

[113]

these are the human values
God's judged fit to reveal His divine values.

"No one snatches My life from Me.
I lay it down Myself;
and because of that, My Father loves Me."[26]
So that we might share His joy—
the joy of loving voluntarily,
of clinging spontaneously—
we had to be free not to bother about Him.

An old woman who'd read Renan's *Vie de Jésus*
and many other "breviaries of skepticism"
declared, "I simply can't believe Christ is God.
If He were, He'd have given me some proof,
for I've wanted so sincerely to believe in Him."
She hadn't wanted to believe at all:
she'd wanted to know,
to discover some fact
that'd satisfy her intellect.
But this is no place for mere intellect.
God's truth isn't something purely rational.
And when we love somebody,
a thousand arguments don't make one proof
nor do a thousand objections make one doubt.
God doesn't force Himself on anyone.
He loves and then waits for our answer.
The only ones who feel His presence
are those who accept that way of doing things,
those values,
those "proofs"—

those inexplicable
proofs—
for "God can be grasped by the heart,
not by reason."

"No one's ever talked like this man before!"[27]
The rough-and-ready police who said that
had been sent to arrest Him,
yet they risked all they had
because of the way He spoke.
Without a moment's hesitation,
they decided to reconsider everything,
to hazard their all:
their job,
their reputation,
their future
and perhaps their religion
(the good old traditional religion
they were virtually repudiating),
and to counter the jeers
of the other men at headquarters
with a laughable,
sentimental,
preposterous reason like
"We couldn't tell Him to stop—
because He spoke too well."

Indeed, no one speaks like this man,
no one loves like Him,
no one forgives like Him.
God alone reaches our hearts like that;

He alone can make us drink so deeply
            of the bitter and the sweet
                        at one and the same time.

We, too, were smitten on some occasion or other.
      One day, we, too, realized
            that He, and He alone, could cure us
            and that in Him we found our real self,
                        came to life,
                        acquired unity
                        and tasted bliss.
      Perhaps it was a certain prayer said with faith
                  or a particular retreat or confession
            that transformed us.
At any rate, we haven't always been insensible.
      We once loved someone who spoke to us movingly of God;
      we used to drop into a certain church
            and felt happier there than anywhere else on earth.
      When we courageously spurned an occasion of sin
                  and remained good despite temptation
                        and generous despite our
                                    environment,
            we sensed we were being helped and inhabited
                  by Someone who approved of us.

The only problem is
            that we didn't remain faithful to those impressions.
      At the age of forty,
            Saint Teresa of Avila was just barely a respectable nun.
      Then, one day, a picture of the wounded Christ
                  that she'd often passed by before

shook her so deeply
    that she never forgot the feelings that arose in her.
As soon as she noticed she was distracted from Him
                    or preoccupied by something
                    else,
    she merely had to recall that moment,
        for she'd kept it alive in her heart by meditation.[28]
There's what makes saints:
    that capacity for faithfulness.
As for us,
        God lavishes the treasures of His heart on us,
            and we squander them with never a second
            thought.

We treat Jesus like those old friends
    we dearly loved in years past
        but have gradually lost track of.
Though we had nothing against them
            and didn't mean to break off,
    we let circumstances drive us apart.
The first thing we knew,
    we stopped writing
        and no longer reread their letters
                or paged through our picture album.
Then we even let slip a chance to meet them again.
The reason?
    We'd become too busy with something else,
        even though it was far less agreeable,
                far less captivating.
Most likely, we'll never love anyone else as we loved them.
    Still, we never think of them

and, if we paused for a minute,
we'd be shocked to realize
that we don't even *care* to see them now.
Renewing our old friendships and loving once more
would entail too many changes,
too much trouble and exertion,
and we've lost our taste for that.

This is what threatens our relationship with God
and sterilizes our spiritual life:
we don't focus our attention on Him,
we don't look forward to meeting Him
or long to see Him.
Yet we can't see God and can't meet Jesus
unless we constantly yearn to behold Him.
He delights in making Himself known to us
but, despite all His power,
He can manifest Himself
only to those who hunger and thirst for Him.
If we don't know God,
it's because we lack that overpowering desire to see Him;
if we don't recognize Him,
it's because our ungrateful hearts have forgotten
everything He's already told us about Himself.
Faith, love and hope consist in remembering,
when darkness overtakes us,
what we saw, felt and understood
when the sun shone bright.

We don't invent God:
He reveals Himself.

We don't give ourselves to Him:
    He's the one who gives Himself.
All He asks is that we receive Him—
        receive Him as He is:
           poor,
           loving,
           hurt by our indifference,
           anxious and attentive
              to all that concerns us.
We look for Him,
    and He's told us to believe He was present all along.
We think we're vanquishing Him,
    and He surrendered so long ago!

Too many people think religion consists
        in what they do for God—
    those poor, puny, pitiful things
      they sometimes manage to do for Him.
Consequently, they find all of religion
           poor, puny and pitiful
      and they trudge along joylessly,
        making wearisome little "sacrifices"
          to draw a bit closer—
            no, not too close!—
        to that Being
          they picture as supreme
            and free from care.
But religion consists
        in what God does for us—
    those great, stupendous things
      He dreams up for us.

God is so good
   that He's the one who draws near.
All He asks
   is that we be astonished by that fact.
      We just have to marvel at it
                        and breathe deeply.
      We'll be religious insofar as we're amazed:
         "The Lord's performed wonders for me."[29]
God's not someone who receives—
      still less, someone who takes.
   He's the one who gives and pardons,
            whose favors we'll sing for all eternity.

Sounds like an easy religion?
Let's not be so sure.
   We hate to be loved for no reason at all,
      because it means admitting
                        we're not worth anything
                           and wouldn't be worth anything
                              without this love
                                 that gives us being;
         it means consenting to be created—
                        to His likeness;
         it means agreeing to vie with this awesome love
                     that weighs and counts nothing
                        but expects everything.
No wonder we're so afraid to take a chance:
   we know right well
      our religion's an irresistible call
         to love the same way—
               with no *if*'s, *and*'s or *but*'s.

Jesus reminded Angela of Foligno,
      "My love for you is no joke."
   Those who've begun to let Him mold them
      know how true that is.

Our religion's unique in that it bids us believe
      God's the one who loved us first.
   "You haven't chosen Me," said Jesus;
            "I've chosen you."[30]
Are we convinced of it?
   It's not simply a matter of granting
      that God loves humanity.
            That's very easy to admit—no problem at all,
                  for the excellent reason that it means nothing.
   No, it's a matter of believing
      that this love is real,
                  therefore concrete
                  and directed to each of us personally.
   "Not a hair falls from your head
      without the Father's knowledge."[31]
   Not an illusion,
   not a proof of fidelity,
   not an instance of enthusiasm and good will,
   not a slip or a loss of grace in us
      but He knows, is moved and affected by it.
Unless we believe that,
unless we live buoyed up by that assurance,
   we haven't yet started to be Christians.

It's the first question we'll be asked on judgment day:
   "Did you believe that God loved you as an individual,

that He knew you,
desired and waited for you
day after day?"
We all feel an invincible repugnance
when it comes to believing this,
but only when we do believe it
will we begin to grasp the mystery.
It's meaningless to affirm that God loves "the other fellow"
if I don't believe He loves me, too;
for only from the fact that He loves me
can I guess how wonderful He is to love the rest of us.
Otherwise, I'm unconsciously giving Him reasons to
love them
("Perhaps they're holy and deserving"),
whereas if I manage to believe He can love even me—
this insufferable creature
I alone have really sized up—
then I'll know
the breadth and length and height and depth
of His unimaginable love.[32]
Saints are those who'll be able to say,
"I've known the love God bore me
and I've believed in it."
But as for us, we'd have to answer,
"I haven't been able to.
Oh, I've often been told so
and I've heard a lot of sermons about it,
but I've always thought
it was just a way of speaking,
a kindly lie,
a pious pat on the back to cheer us."

There's the difference between the saints and us.
Yet no one can measure more accurately than they
the inadequacy,
the frightful powerlessness of mankind
to enter into God's plans
and the heaped-up refusals that block our way to Him.

C. S. Lewis writes:
"Perhaps you have imagined that this humility in the
saints is a pious illusion at which God smiles. That is
a most dangerous error. It is theoretically dangerous,
because it makes you identify a virtue (*i.e.*, a perfection) with an illusion (*i.e.*, an imperfection), which
must be nonsense. It is practically dangerous because
it encourages a man to mistake his first insights into
his own corruption for the first beginnings of a halo
round his own silly head. No; depend on it, when the
saints say that they—even they—are vile, they are
recording truth with scientific accuracy."[33]

If that's true,
how can God love us,
and why?
What does it all mean?

It's important to have a clear understanding of this,
since the essence of religion lies in being convinced
that God's interested in what we do.
True atheism consists in thinking the opposite
and being resigned to the idea.

An atheist is one who goes through life
experiencing, encountering and suffering
all sorts of things
as if he didn't believe God cares.
According to this definition,
how many of us are atheists!

We imagine we've a right to despise ourselves heartily.
We won't acknowledge our duties toward the being
that was entrusted to us from the first.
We don't really believe
there's something in us to respect and safeguard,
something God cherishes—even if we don't.
We feel we can expend our ill-temper on that being,
whom at least God loves
because He invented it.
What we have to do is to stop confusing self-hatred
and humility.
We must be willing to communicate
with that invention,
with the will of God which every one of us is.
That's the first form of faith, hope and charity
God demands of us,
and it's what we usually refuse to give Him
till our dying breath.
Only in the last lines of his diary,
a few minutes before his death,
could Bernanos' country priest write:
"I'm reconciled to myself now,
to this poor shell of me.
How easy it is to hate ourselves!

True grace makes us forget ourselves, instead.
Yet if pride were dead in us,
   the supreme grace would be to love ourselves
      in all humility,
         as we'd love any suffering member
            of Jesus Christ."

What does God love in us?
Certainly not our worth.
   If we thought so,
      we'd soon find ourselves repeating the Pharisee's prayer.
         And we know what Jesus thought of that,
            even though it was full of *thank you*'s.
Surely not the name *Catholic,* either.
   Jesus had a yearning to reach the heathen,
      those who didn't give Him a piece of their mind
            in the name of "religious principles,"
      those who weren't so sure their judgment was correct
         and who'd come to realize
               He might see things more clearly
                  than they.
   He loved those fresh, open minds,
         those enthusiastic hearts,
      whose power to believe hadn't been dulled
         by long-standing habit.
Neither does God love us because of our sins.
   "He upbraided them for their hardness of heart,"[34]
      as He does us for resisting His call.
   He loved Mary Magdalene,
      but she'd changed right from their first meeting.
   The rich young man who turned away,

appalled at Christ's exigencies,
never became His friend.

God loves those to whom He can give most,
those who expect most from Him,
who are most open to Him,
need Him most
and rely on Him most for everything.
Little He cares
whether they're as pure as Saint John
or as sinful as Mary Magdalene
or Zacchaeus.
All that matters to Him
is that they like to depend on Him,
to rejoice in Him
and live through Him alone.
God loves the humility,
the responsiveness,
the wholesomeness
of people who are sincere enough to know
they're not very loveable
and yet simple enough to believe
He loves them
and will give their glad hearts
whatever they need.
He loves those who realize
they're just bumps on a log
but feel nonetheless sure
they'll do something great—
because God moves mountains
when we ask Him to,

with faith.

That, above all, is the spirit of poverty:
   the ability to be shaken and uprooted,
   the eager and constant readiness to be moved—
      emotioned and set in motion—
         by God's loving power.

This activity of His most often occurs
   in a place we can't enter,
   at the very root of our being,
for that's where God reaches us,
    where He operates,
      molds us
       and ceaselessly perfects
        His work in us.
We please Him to the extent that we let Him act there.

Man still needs to be created almost entirely.
   "My Father's always working, and so am I"[35]—
    which is another way of saying,
   "I go on creating endlessly.
   I continually bear,
       and bear with,
         the eternal children you are."
God alone knows us as we are inside
   and He alone'll love us
     even though we lose all our qualities,
   because He loves,
      not our qualities,
      but us.
Only He will put up with us forever.

God alone knows
  what He expects of us,
  what response He's looking for
  and how many people's destinies depend on ours.
When we scorn ourselves,
  we scorn all those plans of His,
      all the dreams He was going to realize
          through us,
      all the joy He anticipated from us
      and all the hope He's placed in us.
Each of us is a piece of property
  that belongs to God
      but is entrusted to us.
 We hardly ever know of what use it is,
  and, as a rule, He's careful not to tell us.
  Quite naturally, we often wonder
      what it can possibly be for
      and who or what can ever really benefit
          from our life.
Faith makes us believe
  that God deems it useful,
              necessary for His projects
              and indispensable to His joy.

When we feel raised above ourselves,
  we know we're deep in God,
          moved by Him,
          and couldn't function at that level without Him.
  Artistic and poetic inspiration give us a sensible idea
      of what happens at such times.
At any rate, we have to be convinced that,

whether we feel it or not,
we're always lifted up, elevated and inspired,
led by His attentive hand
and watched over by His unchanging love.

To believe in God's love
is to believe that He's passionately interested
in each of us personally
and continually.
If we're convinced of that,
how can we fail to respect the sons or daughters
He loves so much in us?
We should be thoroughly ashamed of the way
we maltreat them.
I don't mean we have to be solemn
about our activity,
our effectiveness,
our eventual success
or even our probable failures.
What we do have to take seriously
is the importance and the weight
God's intervention gives these things.
The most efficacious deed we can perform is prayer,
for it's in the active passivity of prayer
that everything's decided
and everything takes shape.
What we seem to accomplish later,
what's actually done through us,
is prepared by God
during those moments of silent, glad assent
in that part of our being

which we're not aware of
and in which everything we'll someday become
takes root
and finds nourishment.
But we can't believe God loves us
without believing His love enhances our worth.
Over-insisting on the idea of gift and gratuitousness
can make us forget the existence of the gift
and what it bestows.

God's love doesn't only make us do
what we couldn't have done before;
it makes us become
what we wouldn't have become without it:
infinitely more open,
more flexible and trusting,
more cheerful and cheering,
more refreshing
than the person we ourselves would've fashioned—
that old, familiar creature whose dismal image
we're determined to preserve—
and, above all, more loving.

"Simon, there's something I want to tell you.
Those who need little forgiveness
feel little love;
but those who need much forgiveness
respond with great love."[36]
Only God knows how to love.
And only those who realize
that they've been forgiven and loved thus

are capable of loving thus themselves.
"Everyone who loves is born of God and knows God."[37]
Only those who've answered His love
by returning and diffusing it
will be invited to enter into it more deeply.
"My sheep know My voice and follow Me."[38]
They won't rest till they've done for another
what God's done for them.
With the same love and the same patience God showed,
they're going to help their neighbor discover in himself
the new being God's awakened in them,
the face He showed them
so they could at last recognize
and accept themselves;
they're going to help someone find out
that he, too, is capable of the perfect fidelity,
gratitude
and love
that were revealed to them.
For Jesus didn't say,
"Love one another,"
but
"Love one another as I've loved you."[39]

FIVE: FORGIVENESS

"O God, You show Your power especially by granting pardon."[1]
People recognized Christ because He remitted sin.
That was the Good News,
the meaning of His advent:
"Go tell everyone his sins can be forgiven!"
Jesus is essentially "the Saviour."
"Where there's much sin,
there's even more grace."[2]
He came, not to abolish sin,
but to forgive it.
"I've come for sinners," He used to say,
"not for the righteous."[3]

Those who couldn't tolerate such mercy rejected Him.
Mohammedans, for instance, refuse to believe
in the divinity of Christ
because they can't accept the idea of a God
who's so "unjust," as they see it—
who doesn't take vengeance on His enemies
but suffers all manner of abuse from them,
who lets the wicked do as they please
and, instead of pulverizing them,
anxiously hopes they'll reconsider returning
to Him.
"There's more joy in heaven over one sinner who repents..."[4]

If this thought fills us with warmth and gladness,
we're close to Christ.
If it annoys and vexes us
or makes us shrug our shoulders in resignation,
that's because we still have none of His spirit.
We're deists, perhaps, but certainly not Christians.
Many of us are Mohammedans
and don't know it.

"God alone can forgive sins."[5]
Above and beyond its juridical meaning,
we must read this statement
as a sort of description of God.
Only He "knows how" to pardon.

We surely don't.
According to the old saw, women forgive
but never forget.
And as for men, they're so self-centered
they forget
and very rarely take time, thought or trouble to forgive.
All in all, human forgiveness is a crushing thing,
an unpleasant memory
we can't shake off.
The superiority of those who grant pardon
utterly quashes those who receive it.
There's forgiveness, but no reassurance,
no consolation,
no encouragement.
God's the only one who can manage
all four together.

You see, forgiving kindly entails humiliating oneself.

The prodigal's father doesn't want to hear another word
about the whole episode.

He gives a banquet.

That's how God does it, too.

He alone can make forgiveness
something glorious to remember.

He's so glad to absolve us
that those who've afforded Him that joy feel,
not like disagreeable, troublesome pests,
but like pampered children,
understood and heartened,
pleasing and useful to Him,
and infinitely better than they thought.

"O happy fault!" they could cry.

"If we weren't sinners
and didn't need pardon more than bread,
we'd have no way of knowing
how deep God's love is."

"Jesus looked at a publican
sitting in the tax-collector's office."[6]

There he was—Matthew,
doing his job,
a crooked job of bleeding the people,
ready to pounce on his next victim.

The fact of sitting at his desk was a confession in itself;
more than that, it was like being caught red-handed.

Jesus said, "Follow Me,"
and, Saint Luke tells us,
"Matthew left everything behind, arose and followed Him."

That's one confession that didn't take long;
    and Matthew did penance right away,
        for *penance* means a change of heart,
            a conversion.
    (Accordingly, the sacrament of forgiveness
        isn't "confession," as we often call it,
            but really "the sacrament of penance.")
There was no need for Matthew to recite his sins.
    All you had to do was look around once,
        see the desk,
            the piles of money stacked up there
                by overcharging and extortion,
            the decent people who stood aloof,
            the emptiness around the notorious den,
            the scorn of passers-by,
    and you soon knew the whole story.

"Follow Me."
    Matthew couldn't get over it:
        being absolved just like nothing,
            in two words,
                right at the scene of his crimes,
            when he'd been reviled, ostracized and spurned
                by everyone with any sense of right
                        and justice.

    And then being called!
        That meant Jesus knew him,
            Jesus was speaking to him,
            Jesus wanted to have him near.
Matthew was beside himself with joy and amazement.

He left everything there—
        forgetting, for the first time in his life,
                to weigh and calculate;
    threw himself into Christ's arms—
        the first that'd ever been open to him;
    and, without hesitating, obeyed the friendly voice
        that spoke to him—
                        obeyed immediately,
                                in front of everybody.
(We, on the contrary, are so timid about confession:
    we go as secretly and rarely as possible,
            lest anyone notice;
    we take fainthearted resolutions
            and prudently restrict them.)
"And Matthew spread a great feast in his home."
    (Will we ever celebrate going to confession
        by giving a merry banquet?
    Just try to imagine asking,
        "What's that big dinner for over at So-and-So's?"
        and being told,
        "Why, he's just been to confession!")

"Many publicans and sinners sat at table
                        with Jesus and His disciples,
        for they were numerous,"
            adds Mark, who always says everything,
    "and they, too, followed Him."[7]
You can visualize the whole scene:
    sinners, all of them
            ("See what happens

[139]

when you open your door to the riffraff?"),
mighty proud
and very much at home.
After all, sinners could be at ease with Matthew:
they'd stolen and gotten rich together
and borne the contempt of good men.
But now, salvation was coming down on them from heaven.
It'd reached Matthew in his office a few hours ago,
so why not all do like him?
Together, they acknowledged their sins;
together, they turned their hearts to God
and feasted.
"Jesus," they said, "is good—
much better than all that money
we're not going to steal any more.
All we want is to remain together like this,
free from guilt
and close to Him."

But the story wasn't going to end there.
Scandal spreads fast among good Christians,
and they do their share to keep it going.
"When the Scribes and the Pharisees saw
that Jesus was eating with sinners and publicans,
they taunted the disciples:
'Why does your master choose to dine with—
people like that?'"
What spite it took to humiliate these sinners
out loud,
without deigning to address them directly,
on the very day of their salvation;

what malice to come slinging mud at them
                and mar the first real joy they'd ever felt!
But, as in the case of Mary Magdalene,
    Jesus couldn't remain indifferent to this cruelty
                            and the pain it caused.
        Though not spoken to, He Himself answered,
                        He Himself defended them:
        "It's not the healthy who need a physician,
                but, rather, the sick."[8]
And Matthew, with good reason, remembered one sentence
            that the other Evangelists forgot.
    It ran: "Go and learn what this means:
                    'I want mercy, not sacrifice.' "[9]

It's easy to imagine how furious the Pharisees must've been.
    They,
        the wise ones,
        the guardians of virtue and orthodoxy,
        the self-appointed directors of souls—
    they'd come to help and enlighten this mad prophet.
            With their long experience,
                they knew the situation
                    and felt morally obliged to tell Him
                        He was in danger.
He seemed not to realize
    there are places you simply don't go,
            people you can't approach
                without contamination;
He ignored elementary prudence and propriety.
    "Go and learn . . ."
        That's how He answered them,

right there, before that ardent band of
"heathen."

Easy, too, to picture how these converted publicans reacted.
They must've waved their arms with noisy delight,
insolent and triumphant,
and, like true Orientals, loosed a torrent of words:
shouts, denunciations and wild promises.

Without question, Jesus'd won the day.
He'd unchained them.
Unchained—there's no other word for it.
He had freed them
from the fetters of their sins
and of "just" men's
obloquy.
Everyone else'd shackled them to their crime,
but Jesus'd come to find them there
and lead them out of it.

"Follow Me."
Never would Matthew forget that moment
when he arose, reeling with bliss.
Whenever Luke, Mark or John mention the Apostles,
they call him Levi or Matthew;
but in his own Gospel
he always refers to himself as "Matthew the
publican"—
glad to keep recalling
how far Jesus'd stooped down to pick him up

and to what length Christ's kindness'd gone
for him,
and acutely conscious
that his sins'd become a "happy fault."

We sometimes see young persons like that nowadays,
for youth is still generous enough to do the same thing.
When college students talk about a professor they admire,
you can hear them laying it on:
"Now, there's a regular guy!
I did such and such a thing to him
and a lot more besides.
Well, he called me into his office and,
believe it or not,
told me he was counting on me.
Imagine that! After everything I'd done . . ."
The next fellow adds his bit:
"Wait till you hear this. I did worse yet."
And, the first thing they know,
their shame's turned into happiness
because they're thinking primarily
of somebody else
and of the goodness
their misdeeds brought into the limelight,
and they're so dazzled
they want to share the revelation with everyone.

In heaven, someday, we'll reminisce, too, and tell each other
how we owe everything
to God's unimaginable mercy and forgiveness.
Our beatitude will lie in witnessing to His love,

not in getting a certificate of merit
for the peevish little virtues
we'll be only too happy not to mention.

As C. S. Lewis says,
"It may be that salvation consists not in the cancelling
of these eternal moments but in the perfected humility
that bears the shame forever, rejoicing in the occasion
which it furnished to God's compassion and glad that
it should be common knowledge to the universe. Perhaps in that eternal moment St. Peter—he will forgive
me if I am wrong—forever denies his Master. If so, it
would indeed be true that the joys of Heaven are for
most of us, in our present condition, 'an acquired
taste'—and certain ways of life may render the taste
impossible of acquisition. Perhaps the lost are those
who dare not go to such a public place."[10]

Spiritually, our future consists,
not in ceasing to view ourselves as sinners,
but in seeing that fact ever more clearly,
accepting it
and rejoicing in God's power
and incredible desire
to rescue us in spite of everything.

We must learn to believe in the Redemption
and take it seriously.
For most of us, being a Christian means thinking
we've been convicted because of someone else's crime
(Adam's or Eve's)

and are now the beneficiaries
of Another's somewhat exaggerated sacrifice.
So we pretend to be very sad about the one
and very glad about the other;
we make believe we're lost
and then make believe we're saved.
But what do we honestly think?
Where would we have been in our element:
in Matthew's house,
sitting at table with the sinners
and the publicans,
or outside with the respectable citizens,
wearing the calm dignity of serious men?

We don't know what God's doing
or what we're doing, either.
We shouldn't, however virtuously, bewail Adam's sin
but deplore the way we tirelessly persist in ours.
The first thing the Holy Spirit does in us,
says Jesus,
is to convince us of our sinfulness.[11]

Suppose someone were to ask us,
"Do you consider yourself a great sinner?"
We'd most probably answer,
"Oh, average—pretty decent, even."
Well, if we're in that respectable middle class—
neither very holy nor very sinful—
we're not the ones Christ came for.
"I've come for sinners, not for the just. . . .
I've come to save those who are lost."[12]

Instead, we're with those
who look at Calvary,
the Cross,
the nails
and all that blood
and secretly feel like protesting,
"Come, now, Lord! This is embarrassing.
There was no need to go so far!"

If we could glimpse the truth, we'd find out
that we're busy fighting Him—
all of us,
all the time,
and that we keep causing and forcing Him
to be racked and crucified—
even
(no! *especially*)
when our conscience is at peace.
Saint Paul though he was doing right
as he kicked against the goad.[18]
Consider all the people in the Gospels who opposed our Lord.
We may as well say everybody did:
Jews and Romans,
rich and poor,
priests and laymen,
pontiffs and the impenitent thief.
Had they formed a pact with the devil?
No, but they were serving him unwittingly—
just as we do—
because he's only too truly the prince of this world,
as Jesus told us.[14]

Without the Redemption, we'd have remained like larvae.
We do evil and think we're doing good—
    or, rather, tell ourselves we are.
Never do we manage to forget and rise above ourselves.
Our faith, hope and charity are frightfully sterile.
We criticize all that God sends our way
    and dread what He has in store for us.
            When do we say, "It had to happen"—
                when all's going well
                    or when everything's out of joint?

If, for an instant, we could see ourselves as we are,
    we'd view this incessant rebellion.
But spiritual insights like that are rare and brief.
That explains why our confessions
                        are such gloomy, joyless affairs.
"Bless me, Father, for I've sinned"
            should be a shout of gladness
                    or a sigh of relief.
We're not saying, "Punish me, Father; yell at me,"
    but "Bless me, Father; celebrate with me;
        for, at last, I understand
            that I've sinned,
            that I was wrong
                and God was right;
        I can finally see that
                if my life was so dismal and burdensome,
            it was my fault, not His.
        Now everything's fine:
            I'm going to change;
            I'm going to let Him change me. . . .

> Here are the things that'll be different
> from now on: . . ."

Listing our sins is meaningless
    unless we're gratefully recalling
            how we've just broken the bonds that held us
        and are asking the priest
            to attest to our new freedom.

Through the words of absolution, God is simply saying,
    "I love you.
    I've wanted to forgive you right along
        and I'm even happier to grant you pardon
            than you are to receive it.
    My son was dead, and now he's come back to life again.
    Let there be a big feast!"

Each confession we make applies the Redemption to us
                personally
                and instantly.
Each return to God prefigures, heralds our definitive return
            on the day of our death.
Each absolution foreshadows and prepares the welcome
        our Father's reserved for us in heaven,
    as He waits with open arms,
            like the father in the parable,
        peering down the road, ready to greet his runaway son.

If we were more convinced that we're sinners,
    we'd have a better idea of how fondly God awaits us,
    we'd know the bliss we're stepping into,

we'd be overjoyed,
our confessions'd be a foretaste of the eternal banquet,
and our Masses, a daily renewal of it.

For the Mass, also, is a rendezvous for God and sinners.
Are we fully aware that that's why we're invited to it?
Reading the missal will amply prove
that only sinners have a right to be there.
If we don't admit our sinfulness,
most of the prayers for Mass
should make us very ill at ease—
unless we've resigned ourselves, once and for all,
to mouthing formulas we don't believe
one bit.

The Confiteor's a confession,
a public confession,
in which, for a change, we're not trying to say,
"There's nothing I can do about it,"
or pinning the blame
on the other fellow,
adverse circumstances
or our temperament.
"*Mea culpa*," we repeat, "*mea culpa*—
yes, it's *my* fault."
For once in our life, we're not looking for excuses.
After that, the priest goes up to the altar and prays,
"Remove our sins, O Lord . . ."
We ask the martyrs to intercede and obtain remission for us:
"Lord, we beseech You,
through those saints whose relics lie here

and through all the saints,
deign to forgive me all my sins.
May it be so!"
The Kyrie pleads for the same grace:
"Have mercy on us!"
Before the Gospel, the celebrant begs to be purified
and, after, kisses the book, imploring,
"May the words of the Gospel blot out our sins."
At the Offertory we say,
"Holy Father, almighty and eternal God,
please accept this spotless offering.
I,
Your unworthy servant,
present it to You,
my true, living God,
in reparation for my countless sins,
offenses
and negligences
and in behalf of everyone who's with me here
and of all the faithful,
living and dead . . ."
Just before the end of the Canon,
after we've recited all the mementos,
we call His attention back to ourselves with the words
"And to us sinners also . . ."
We're about to communicate,
feed on God's bread;
but we who'll receive it are sinners.
It's Matthew's banquet all over again,
to the perpetual horror of the "good,"
who gasp, "He eats with sinners!"

"Lamb of God, You who take away the sins of the world,
    have mercy on us. . . .
Lord Jesus," we entreat, "don't look on my sins
      but on the faith of Your Church. . . .
Lord Jesus, by Your most holy Body and Blood
      deliver me from all my transgressions. . . .
Lord Jesus, I dare receive Your Body,
      though I don't deserve to. . . .
O Lord, I'm not worthy. . . ."

Evidently, we've no idea what we're saying.
    We'd have a fit
      if the priest,
        overhearing us and wishing to respect our scruples,
      passed us by at Communion time
      and invited us to confession first.
    We'd rant and rave
      if somebody once seemed to believe our protestations.
All our prayers are horribly empty,
                 stereotyped,
                 mechanical.
    We go through the versicles and the responses;
    we recite;
    and the unworthier we say we are,
      the worthier we feel—automatically.
        (My, such humility!)
We humble ourselves in the same spirit
    in which we take the last place—
        hoping, that is, to be given the first,
      as when the host in the Gospel says,
        "My friend, come up here next to me."[15]

What a calamity
    if the other fellow missed his cue
                and left us standing there
                    openmouthed
                      as though we'd said the obvious,
    or if the priest agreed that it's quite true:
        we're really not worthy!
How unfair,
    taking advantage of our self-abasement
        to abase us further still!
        "Well! I'll never set foot in that church again!"
At Mass, as in every phase of our existence,
    we pretend to believe we're sinners.
All we can do, consequently,
    is pretend to believe we've been forgiven.
As a result,
    our whole spiritual life's nothing but pseudo contrition
                and pseudo bliss.

How can we get out of this living death,
                this barren, dreary sham?
By no longer straining for the sort of virtue
    that'd just be another source of pride,
by fathoming the lowliness we talk about,
by believing that that's where God'll start working wonders,
by finding our happiness in His gifts,
by delighting,
        not because we're strong (even in virtue),
        but because we're starved for Him,
           because we've been taken down a peg,
           because we're among those little ones

He Himself'll raise to His own heart,
because we're publicans
just like Matthew.

On the other hand, we mustn't be cynical and say,
"If religion's only for the wicked,
I'm going to keep on sinning for all I'm worth.
The more the better:
it makes me religious,
it gets me ready for Mass
and able to serve God.
A few more sins, and I'll be all set;
then I can say those prayers in the missal
with genuine feeling:
'I've sinned in thought, word and deed—
I certainly have!
Therefore, I beg you . . .'
No, I won't have to fake it any more.
I'm going to be a real sinner, I am—
an honest-to-badness Christian—
not like all those hypocrites
who think they're something
because they felt obliged to practice a little virtue
before coming to church."
Of course, that'd be disastrous, too.

Holiness is like humility—very strange:
the moment we think we have it,
we lose it.

To be a Christian means

to feel as uncomfortable in sin as in virtue.
"The Son of Man has no place to lay His head."[16]
A true Christian *should* feel like a hypocrite.
We have to say something good now and then,
even if only to encourage others.
But if we talk that way,
they may imagine we act accordingly;
and if we do good once in a while,
they may think we *are* good.
Now, we're all painfully conscious that what we are
sometimes flatly contradicts what we do.
In fact, we often do good
to compensate some particularly glaring defect
we've just uncovered.

In a word,
we're ill at ease in virtue
because we know it's only a borrowed cloak
that could easily be hiding an imposter,
and ill at ease in sin
because it separates us from God.
How can we be sincere in such a dilemma?

The outspoken frankness of the present day is no solution.
"I don't like So-and-So;
but I'm not going to put on an act
like everybody else;
I'm not going to pretend or try,
like a hypocrite,
to overcome a natural antipathy."

This attitude sounds sincere,
    but it's dangerously deceptive.

Nothing is so false
        as defining ourselves in terms of our activity,
            identifying ourselves with what we do.
The whole picture's inexact: both the black and the white,
                        the right and the wrong.
There's a big difference between us and our actions:
        we're worse than the good we do
            and better than the bad.
Besides our inclination to mediocrity,
    we have a still more persistent tendency
                    to rise above it,
                    to get up every time we fall,
            and an unflagging desire
                to improve.
That, too, is our self,
                part and parcel of us—
            as much as the evil we do.
Genuine sincerity consists,
    not in concluding that we're bad,
    but in affirming that we're a blend of good and bad
                    and aren't happy about it.
Genuine sincerity's a willingness
    to make something of ourselves
    and not accept ourselves ready-made.
Beyond a certain age, it takes more humility
    to note cheerfully
        that we're progressing a bit
    than to declare,

with all the learned authors of the day,
that we're a hopeless mixture of good and evil drives.

"Follow Me!"
   Leaving everything behind,
      Matthew got up and followed Him
         and made a splendid feast in his home,
     with the same simplicity,
       the same humble astonishment
       and trust
         that made Zacchaeus say,
      "Lord, this is what I'm going to give from now on . . ."[17]

The most characteristic feature about us
   is this dynamic urge to progress constantly,
     this inexorable call,
     this "vocation,"
       which is repeated so often that,
         eventually,
       it becomes a more integral part of us
        than are the opposite forces.

Only when we acknowledge this dual pull
    can we come near the truth about ourselves.
When Saint Paul thought he was attaining holiness,
      he wrote,
    "I'm not the one who's living any more:
      it's Christ who's living in me."[18]
And when he noticed he wasn't holy, he confessed,
    "I can't understand what's happening:
      I don't do what I wish

but what I hate. . . .
I don't do the good I want
but the wrong I abhor. . . .
When I try to do what's right,
evil's breathing down my neck;
for my heart delights in God's commandments,
but my flesh wars against my mind—
law against law—
and subjects me to the rule of sin
that holds sway in my members.
How unhappy I am!
Who'll deliver me from this body
that only brings me death?
The grace of God, through Jesus Christ
our Lord."[19]

"I sense that there are two men in me."
That's the truth Paul discovered about himself,
and it holds good for each of us.
But Christ lifts us high above this evil
and helps us break loose from our worst faults.
"The just?
I haven't come for them.
I've come to call sinners,"
and Saint Luke adds "to repentance."[20]

We'll achieve genuine sincerity by humbly rejoicing
in this constant upward climb,
in this ever-pressing but never-failing help,
and in the fact that we're sinners,
but sinners who are always forgiven

and always raised far above
our sins.
Then we'll be able to adopt the right attitude,
without cynicism or hypocrisy;
we'll conform to the truth,
without rejecting,
under the pretext that we're sinners,
the best part of ourselves—
that part which we don't make
but which slowly makes us over
to God's image.

"Why are you downcast, O my soul,
and why troubled within me?
Trust in God,
for I'll praise Him forever!"[21]
Our whole existence moves back and forth in this dialogue;
our whole life oscillates between these two poles
but is gradually magnetized by the stronger one:
"Trust in God.
I'll praise Him forever,
for He's my Saviour and my God."

If Matthew seems so glad to repeat that he was "the publican,"
that's because
it's his way of telling Jesus over and over,
"You're my Saviour and my God";
his way of reminding himself and us,
"If you only knew how badly I needed
to be saved
and what miracles

of redemption,
penance
and conversion
the Lord worked in the baseness of my heart!"
The more we're forgiven,
the more we love.

"At daybreak, Jesus came into the Temple again,
and all the people drew near Him.
As He was sitting there, teaching,
the Scribes and the Pharisees dragged a woman in,
stood her in the middle of the group
and said to Him,
'Master, this woman's just been caught in adultery.
The Law of Moses commands us
to stone the likes of her.
But You—what do You say?' "[22]

If we use a little imagination and relive this scene
with those who were present,
we'll feel the almost inhuman cruelty of it all.
There she was:
a woman,
quite alone,
haled in by a band of "just" men,
who brought her through the crowd,
placed her in their midst,
told the entire story
and bared her shame before everyone—
all so that they might test Jesus

and have something
to accuse Him of.
He, too, was quite alone
and entirely at their mercy.
Realizing this was a rare chance to catch Him,
they craftily set their trap.
If He condemned her,
He'd lose that reputation for understanding
and kindness,
gentleness
and mercy,
which drew simple hearts
and gave Him a jubilant escort
of converted sinners.
If He didn't condemn her,
why, that'd be better yet:
serious men'd have their eyes opened once for all
and would start asking,
"How long can this go on?
You people who are married and have daughters,
you who prize honor, the home
and the family—
do you still agree
with that so-called prophet of yours,
a preacher who encourages
adultery?"

It was such a sorry spectacle
that Jesus didn't even look at the accusers
but stooped over and wrote on the ground
with His finger—

words of discouragement, perhaps,
weariness
or disgust.
But the Scribes and the Pharisees wouldn't let go
and insisted that He answer;
so He straightened up and replied,
"Let the one who's sinless among you
throw the first stone."
Then He bent over again and resumed writing
on the ground;
and, with His answer ringing in their ears,
they slinked away,
one by one,
beginning with the eldest.

One look,
one encounter,
one word from Jesus,
and they all beheld their sinfulness.
They understood, they saw,
in an instant,
that Jesus knew everything about them
and that, if He chose, He could reveal
how and when,
with whom and how often
they'd sinned.
A few minutes before, they'd made a grand entry,
puffed up with arrogance and hypocritical indignation,
but, oh, how shamefacedly they left!
Their exit was tantamount to a public confession.
And it's not too likely that the onlookers held their tongues.

They must've commented and given their opinion,
        trying to put two and two together
        and cracking a few good jokes.
The would-be denouncers could've kicked themselves
        for starting the whole business.
But Jesus didn't browbeat them:
        He simply told them what He had to say
        and went back to writing on the ground.
        Their discomfiture saddened Him
        as much as the woman's blistering disgrace,
        and everything about the incident
        appeared mean and ugly and distressing.

He was left alone,
        with the woman still standing there.
Raising Himself, He asked,
        "Where've they gone?
        Hasn't anyone condemned you?"
She answered, "No one, Lord,"
        but there was no triumph in her voice.
Jesus' words, anyway, sounded less like a question
                       than a statement
                            of fact;
        it was as if He'd said,
            "No one's free from sin,
                but it's too bad they had to find out this way.
            Where are they now?"
Then He concluded,
        "I won't condemn you, either.
            Go home now, and don't sin any more."

Of course, she wouldn't.
How could she possibly want to?
She'd be forever protected by the glance
that'd saved her from the stones of the mob.
Accompanied, encouraged and inspired
by the thought of His kindness and sympathy,
she'd no longer need to fill her life with sin.
For all time to come,
her heart was full of gratitude, love and joy.
She was going away pardoned,
not judged.
She'd met Christ, the Son of the living God,
and never would He desert her now.
He'd graciously forgiven her—
graciously granted her the grace,
the gift,
of forgiveness.

In a few seconds,
she'd learned what it really means to love
and be loved;
at one and the same time,
Christ'd shown her what love is
and kindled it in her heart.
She was going away forgiven,
and those who are forgiven much
love much.
What she found out
and what we perceive in our more profitable confessions
is that we've been mentioning the wrong sin.
Our real crime wasn't what we thought—

not those insipid acts that helped us kill time
(after all, we had to do something
to beguile our emptiness).
No, our real crime was
that we didn't honestly think there was Someone
who could satisfy our hunger
and quench our thirst forever;
we didn't know who that Someone was,
and we didn't dare believe in a love
so compelling
that it made all our imitations
unnecessary.

How'll we know whether God's forgiven us?
We'll be able to tell if,
after going to confession one day,
we feel,
as Matthew did,
that we've left everything behind—
almost without realizing it.
The reason is
that we'll finally have let Him touch us,
we'll have answered His terrifying call
to change and disarm,
to give,
to pardon and ask pardon,
to speak the truth
and grow equally aware
of our immense poverty
and our infinite possibilities.
"Leaving everything, Matthew followed Him."

SIX: THE HOLY SPIRIT

"My going will be advantageous to you."[1]
    That's what Jesus said before leaving us.
    That's how He announced
               and, with His foresight, evaluated
      the last way He'd chosen to meet us,
      the final rendezvous,
      the everlasting tryst He was setting with each of us
            for all eternity.

"Listen! I'm with you till the end."[2]
        Do we believe it?
        Do we really think we've gained something?
"If I don't go,
    the Paraclete won't come to you;
  but if I do go,
    He, the Spirit of truth, will come
               and teach you everything."[3]
        Do we take these words as a promise
                    or a mere pious
                      consolation?
        Do we read them as poetry
                or fact?

Have we ever sensed the nearness of this Paraclete,
                  this Spirit of truth,

this promised
companion?
"He's the one who makes us call out, 'Abba! Father!' "⁴
Still, how often have we fully realized we have a Father?
How often have we truly felt we're sons—
sons of God?

And yet, without the Spirit,
religion'd be just a flat, barren code
of obligations,
empty prayers,
fruitless sacraments
and boring Masses.
It's He who makes us taste the things of God
and savor their sweetness.
But do we actually delight in them?
"O God, You've taught the hearts of Your faithful
by the breath of the Holy Spirit.
Grant us, then, by that same Spirit,
ever to relish the things of God
and always enjoy His consoling presence.
This we beg through Jesus Christ our Lord.
So let it be!"⁵

Who cares to know everything that's going on in a family
except the children that belong to it?
Strangers couldn't care less,
but the children are interested
in all that happens to their father.
Unless we have the adoptional Spirit of God,
His concerns mean nothing to us
and leave us apathetic.

Like the people Saint Paul was trying to convert,
      so many Christians could exclaim,
        "We never even heard there was a Holy Spirit!"[6]
Oh, they've spoken His name, of course—
      hundreds of times, with *Amen* tagged on.
But have they ever once realized
    that they were talking
        about the very principle of their life
  and that the one they were naming
      at that moment
    was the same one who'd opened their lips
      so they could name Him?
When you think of all those poor cold hearts
    and the equally cold sermons that bid them
        perform their Easter duty!
Have they ever been told
    that there is a Holy Spirit—
        the Spirit of love and joy,
          of giving and sharing
          and of brotherly interchange;
  that they're invited to enter into that Spirit
        and communicate with Him;
  that He wants to keep them together
        with their brethren,
        forever,
        in a body;
  that that's what we call "the Church";
  and that that's what they have to discover
    if they're really to perform their Easter duty?

When Saint Paul contrasts the life of the flesh

with the life of the spirit
(living by the Spirit),
he says we can't possibly belong to Christ
unless we change our everyday living.
"Whoever lacks the Spirit of Christ
can't belong to Him."[1]
Just as the Holy Spirit was the origin and the principle
of Christ's incarnation in the womb of the Virgin Mary,
so He's the origin and the principle
of Christ's incarnation in each Christian.
His indwelling in us is as real as the Incarnation;
and the historical incarnation perdures
and attains its goal
by spiritualizing the whole of humanity.

Pentecost proved
that God had become flesh,
not for thirty-three years,
but for all time;
and that He'd shared with us
the very thing that constitutes His life—
in other words, His Spirit of love—
forever.
Pentecost inaugurated
the irrevocable and perpetual presence of Christ
in the world.

But where?
In your humanity and mine.
That's where He now continues His work
of incarnation

and redemption:
the incarnation of God
and the redemption of the world.

The indwelling of Jesus' Holy Spirit in our hearts
is something more important
than the historical incarnation.
Pentecost was a more earth-shaking event than Christmas.
The Incarnation means
that God became man,
whereas Pentecost means
that man's been invited to become God.
Not only has God stooped down to us
but He wants to lift us all the way up to Himself.
The Spirit's coming was far more resplendent than Christ's.
The incarnation took place at night
in the seclusion of a cave,
while Pentecost blazed forth in broad daylight
with hundreds of people to witness
the transformation.
This was no longer God,
submerged in anguish,
becoming man;
but a whole group of men,
bathed in light and bliss,
becoming God.
"You'll do greater things than I,"[8]
Jesus'd promised, with His Church in mind.

The Church is the specific work of the Spirit.
"If only you knew the gift God's given you!"[9]

[171]

Well, it's the Church—"the gift of God most high."[10]
We may describe the Church as God existing for man
in man,
God imparted to man.
Now, what's the best thing about God?
His Spirit—Love,
and He associates us with that Spirit
and shares Him with us.
And from the concourse of those who've received Him
the Church comes into being and grows.

Christ wasn't planning to send His Spirit of love
and then disappear.
Rather, He promised us what'd bring us closest to Him.

Where are we supposed to find Him?
The Father revealed Himself in the Old Testament,
where we see Him disowned and betrayed.
"At different times and in different ways,
He spoke to our fathers by the prophets."[11]
But Jerusalem killed the prophets,
"beat one, murdered another and stoned a third....
Finally, He sent them His Son."[12]
The Son revealed Himself in the New Testament
and, in doing so, revealed the Father.
"Whoever sees Me, sees the Father, too."[13]
Then the Spirit was sent to us, in the Church, and revealed
both the Father and the Son
as well as the love He Himself quickens
by the spirit of adoption,[14]

which not only manifests the Trinity to us
but even makes us enter into it.

After announcing the advent of the Spirit,
Christ prayed,
"Father, as You're in Me, so may I be in them!"[15]
That's the Holy Spirit's mission.
"May they all be one, as You and I, Father, are one."[16]
And that's the task
of the Church
and of all those who,
like Mary,
have let the Word take flesh in them—
all those in whom the Holy Spirit begets
a "new man"
because they've acquiesced
and allowed themselves
to be pervaded
by this spirit of interchange and love,
this spirit of communion.

The Holy Spirit gives life to the Church.
It's He who ceaselessly re-creates her
and tirelessly gathers her together
from the four winds.[17]
It's He who causes people to love each other
in spite of everything.
"Don't grieve the Holy Spirit,
in whom you've been sealed. . . .
Be kind to one another
and live in charity."[18]

"All who are led by the Spirit of God
            are the sons of God."[19]
And those who cut themselves off
            from the communion of the brethren—
            from the spirit of communion—
        are no longer sons.
Wherever two or three group together in His name,
            there He'll be,
                in their midst,
                always.[20]
"In His name" means "in His Spirit."
        The purpose is always the same:
                "Father, may they be one in Us."
            There's no efficacious communion
                except in Them,
            but there's no efficacious union with Them
                except in communion.
        The many must grow into one.

That's the import of Ezechiel's beautiful prophecy
            of the parched bones.
"That day, the hand of the Lord laid hold of me.
    He carried me away, in spirit,
        set me down in the middle of a plain covered
                with bones
        and made me walk all around them where they lay,
            countless and completely dried out.
    The Lord said to them,
        'Look! I'm going to send My Spirit into you again,
            and you'll live.
            Then you'll know that I'm the Lord.'

At that, the bones came together,
                    each one fitting into its own joint,
            and sinews and flesh molded them into a whole.
But there was still no spirit in them.
And the Lord commanded me to prophesy
                    and tell the spirit,
        'Listen, this is what the Lord God commands:
            "Come, Spirit, like the wind
                    from the four corners of the world,
                and breathe upon these dead
                    so they may live again."'
And there they were—
        standing on their feet, like a vast army.
Then the Lord said to me,
        'Son of man, these bones represent the house of Israel.
            They lament,
                "Our bones are parched,
                our hope's dead
                and we're lost."'
So He ordered me to prophesy and announce
            what He, the Lord God, promised them:
        'I'll unseal your tombs,
            lead you out of your sepulchers,
                        out of your isolation and discouragement,
                            your sterility and powerlessness—
                    out of everything
                            that walls you up within
                                    yourselves—
            and I'll lead you back into the land of Israel,
                where people love and communicate
                                with one another

and are happy only when sharing.
When I've put my Spirit into you
and you've lived,
enjoying the repose I'll give you
in your own land,
then you'll know who I am.'"[21]

The exact opposite of the turmoil of Babel,
that repose is the joy of Pentecost—
the joy of all those Pentecosts
when men suddenly start
to really love
and understand each other.

What makes us intelligible to everyone?
Love.
"Each heard them speaking in his own language"[22]—
no linguistic feat, this,
no super Berlitz;
just proof that love makes us such
that every man feels he's understood,
cherished,
happy,
close to us.

"You don't know of what spirit you are."[23]
His is the one that'll send us out toward our fellow men
with enthusiasm.
Saint Paul was inspirited
and immediately went to seek the others,
had Ananias pray over him

and followed the rites
of the community.
He who's been described
as having broken his way into apostlehood
perceived at once
that he had to join the others promptly
and enter into communion
with them.

We must be careful not to take the Spirit's title of Comforter
and warp its meaning to suit our individualism—
our sin, in other words.
During our Lord's stay with them,
the Apostles were shaken up more often than consoled.
The only consolation is to love.
We're often galled by the "ingratitude" of people,
but we mustn't go marching off by ourselves every time
to some cozy little chapel,
where we can air our grievances to the Lord
and have the Holy Spirit soothe us
because we don't love each other.
It's only through love
that we have access to the Spirit of Love,
and His consolation consists
in perpetually enabling us to love one another
all over again.

"His task," writes Père Congar,
"isn't enlightening this man or that,
but animating and building up the Body of Christ.
For that reason,

His gifts and His work are essentially communitive.
He operates through the mutual love of the faithful,
a spirit of brotherly love and fellowship."
Moehler, the German theologian, adds:
"Without the influence exercised on us
by the community of the faithful
under the impulsion of the Holy Spirit,
we could neither live a Christian life
nor know our religion."

The Holy Spirit,
who makes the Father go out toward the Son
and the Son toward the Father,
must also make us go out toward one another.

What trouble we have adoring an incarnate God!
When reciting the Creed,
we genuflect as the priest says "was made man";
and during the Last Gospel,
we do the same at the words "was made flesh."
Yes, He became man:
He became—
let's face it—
this neighbor who keeps us from praying well.
But we're not really praying
if we turn our back on Him
and seek Him where He's not to be found:
in our solitary retreat
and our spiritual introversion.
We like to shut everyone out securely
and play "Jesus and I alone in the world,"

or bury our head in our hands
to enjoy our own little holy spirit
undisturbed.
Lucky the deaf, dumb and blind:
they can't notice the harsh cries of this flesh
in which it hardly seems credible
that the Word would've got involved.
We also kneel when we recite *Veni, Sancte Spiritus*
at the Mass for Pentecost.
That's because it's the Incarnation again.
He took on this clay of ours,
and we're asked to be so astonished by that fact
that we have to drop to our knees
when talking about it.
If we reject God in man, we're lost.
Our so-called spirituality's a direct offense
against the Spirit,
who's supposed to teach us "all those things"
that started with the Incarnation.

We belong to Christ only by belonging to others.
Does the host we fervently adore
sometimes make us think of those who'll eat it?
Our veneration falls short
if we offer it to the Head
but refuse it to His members.
Bread's meant to be eaten,
and this Body's the sign and source of another Body,
the Mystical Body,
whose care, honor and vitality
are incumbent on us.

Through baptism,
    we were incorporated
                and bound up with innumerable brothers;
    for us,
        adhering to God supposed we started adhering to them.
He commanded us to love, not only Him,
                       but each other, too;
He wanted us to become God for everyone,
        to resemble Him,
                who never wished to be alone.

God is communitarian.
    He wasn't God before being triune.
From all time,
    God was several,
              a society of Persons
        who know and love one another so well
           that They're infinitely transparent and united.
They had to be several
             to be God;
They had to be together
             to be Themselves;
They had to be sundry
             to be Love.
    "Not in the oneness of a single person,"
                we chant in the Preface of the Holy Trinity;
        and what we mean is,
        "How wonderful that You're not solitary,
                that You're several, instead,
                that You're Love!"

When man was created,
    he was fashioned in the image of God,
        constituted male and female[24]—
    in other words,
        capable of loving,
        but incapable of satisfying himself,
            sufficing unto himself
            or living wholly for himself.
Destined to give himself,
    he can find fulfillment and happiness only in others.
Made to prefer himself in them
            rather than in his own being,
    he can know and love himself better
        when someone frees him from his ego
            and shows him his true nature.

When we communicate,
    we communicate with others.
        And we have to swallow them all
            along with the host;
            otherwise, we won't digest it,
                and it'll stay on our stomach.
    We first have to go and make peace with our brothers
        before we can hope to commune with God
            at the altar.[25]

When we confess our sins,
    we receive pardon
            only if we agree to pass it on;
    we're forgiven

only if we forgive,
and reconciled to God
only if we're reconciled to our fellow men.
We bear the same relation to God
as we bear to others:
we're no closer to Him
than we are to them.

Like any other religious practice,
our confessions mean nothing
unless they're community-wide, so to say.
That's why it's not enough to avow our sins before God
in private prayer.
Some Protestants think Catholics look to absolution
for a feeling of reassurance,
and they explain,
"We don't need that.
We trust in God's goodness
and confess to Him alone."
But Catholics, too, trust in God's goodness—
or, at least, they should.
Theology manuals all agree that perfect contrition
(that is, sorrow for having displeased God)
certainly draws down divine forgiveness
even before sacramental confession's
been completed.
We don't go acknowledge our sins
to somebody who represents God
so as to be "surer" we're pardoned.
We do it because the Word became flesh
and we've offended Him

in that same flesh.
"Whatever you've done to one of these,
the least of My brothers,
you've done it to Me."[26]
For the same reason,
we have to be reconciled to Him
through another man,
who represents the community
while representing Him.

When Jesus said, "I'm giving you a new commandment,"[27]
He didn't mean the content was new.
People'd been repeating
"and your neighbor as yourself"[28]
for ages.
In fact, that was the second commandment.
What was new and dramatic was the importance
He gave it:
"like the first."[29]
They were one and the same precept:
"You've done it to Me."[30]
He bade us love Him in our neighbor.
"My dear ones, let's love one another,
for love's from God;
and anyone who loves is born of God
and knows Him."[31]
Accordingly,
if those who confess to God alone opened their ears,
they might hear Him answer,
"My friend, you're knocking at the wrong door.
It's not here in heaven

that you hurt and grieved and scorned Me;
it's in My Body, rather—
in your fellow men.
Go straighten matters out with them.
This 'direct' reparation's just a bit too easy."

People imagine they've done everything
once they've inventoried their conscience
and scraped every corner clean.
The truth is, they haven't done a thing.
Penance—the sacrament of penance—means
resuming life in common,
re-establishing contact,
expressing our contrition before the community
and, by the admission of our guilt, formulating our desire
to re-enter into fellowship with our brothers
through Eucharistic Communion,
which is ordained to communion
with the whole Church.

At the last judgment, we'll be asked,
not what we've done to the Eucharistic Body of Christ,
but what we've done to His Body, period.
"How many holy hours have you made?"
We can't hope to draw that question—
unless it's asked to underline our hypocrisy
("Not those who cry, 'Lord, Lord!'
but those who do something . . ."[32]).
We know exactly what to expect.
It's one of the clearest texts in the Gospels.[33]
"I was hungry, thirsty and cold," God will say,

"but you didn't pay any attention to Me.
I rang your doorbell one morning,
        when you'd just returned from Mass,
but I was dirty and tired and rough-looking—
      the way men appear when they're
            really down-and-out.
You didn't think it wise to let Me in:
      everything around was clean—
          your entrance hall,
          your children,
          your soul. . . .
So you gave Me a little money—
    a bit more than people usually give,
      lest your conscience bother you
      and lest you feel you owed Me something
        if ever you remembered Me later—
and then you shut your door.
All in all, that's a good way to be greedy
             and still be robbed,
    for nine out of ten such callers are cheats.
Well, I took your money,
      but you remained avaricious of your time,
                    attention
                    and interest.

You should've known Me for what I was
        and kept Me from swindling you.
You should've shown enough clear-sighted understanding
    that I could dare be honest with you.
        (The poor realize that, most of the time,
          no one believes or bothers with them
            unless they make up a fantastic story.)

And even if I were a professional fraud,
you should've guessed that I hide
not only within the poor
but within sinners, too.
You were supposed to find Me there.
Oh, you missed Me day after day,
every day.
You'd heard it said you could find Me
in putting up with your neighbor,
but you didn't suspect that could be so difficult."

And we'll stand there sputtering,
"Lord, do You mean to say that was You—
the fat man who came that day?
But he was bald and everything!
How about that irritating old woman?
She'd certainly had a rough life. . . .
And she was You, even so?
Then that silly curate
who liked to hear himself talk
and always popped up when he shouldn't—
that was You, too?
Why, he was enough to make people
hate the Church!"

The Lord has many surprises in store for us.
One day, two young ladies were returning
from a monastery
where they'd spent Holy Week.
Everything'd been so nice:
the services so beautiful,

the liturgy so actual,
the readings so significant.
They'd sung in Latin and in French,
prayed
and felt thoroughly renewed.
Even now, driving home in their car,
they were still deeply moved by the experience.
Night was falling,
and the road cut across a forest,
miles from the nearest village.
Suddenly, their headlights picked out a man
lying by the roadside:
a tramp, to all appearances,
too weak to drag himself.
The girls wondered whether he was sick,
injured, dying—
or drunk, perhaps.
He might even be playing possum
to assault and rob kindhearted motorists.
Out there, far from everything,
on a deserted stretch of road—
this could very well be a trap:
maybe there were men watching
in the nearby woods,
ready to jump out
as soon as the car stopped
or even slowed down.
The driver stepped on the accelerator
and fled the brewing nightmare.
Quite safe now,
they didn't even stop at the first village

to tell someone about the man
or obtain help for him,
as prudence would've dictated.
They simply pretended they hadn't seen him.
But, somehow, they couldn't talk about the services
any more
and, by the time they'd reached home,
they knew they'd bungled Holy Week.
They'd spent three days pitying Someone
who suffered and was left alone and uncared for,
whose condition brought tears to their eyes
and whom no one thought of comforting.
And when they met Him,
minutes later,
they didn't recognize Him.

Our real guilt can best be gauged,
not by what we do,
but by what we fail to do.
Our indifference to others offends God and His Holy Spirit
infinitely more than the mistakes we happen to make
while on our way to Them.
The reason we can commit all these sins
is that we reject God's invitation to receive
and communicate Love.
Our basic sin is one of refusal:
a refusal to become interested in others
and go out toward them,
a refusal to be touched by their distress,
to help
and sympathize with them.

Ultimately,
    it's a refusal to let the Holy Spirit live and act in us,
        although God wanted to share Him with us.
According to the Gospels,
    the sin against the Spirit
        is the only one that won't be forgiven.
Of course, it won't.
    How can you give Life to somebody
        who refuses to live,
        who hasn't that fundamental desire to live?
    The only life God can give us is His own,
        and that consists in loving—with an active love.
            "My Father works constantly."[84]
    As the Gospels fairly shout on every page,
        doing nothing is what'll damn us.

Take the parable of the talents, for example.
    What did the man with a single talent do?
        He saved it,
            took good care of it,
            spared his meager resources.
    And he lost his soul.
    "But I didn't do anything wrong," he must've argued;
        "my talent's still nice and clean,
                shiny
                and absolutely spotless."
    Still, he went down to hell,
        for he'd sinned against the Holy Spirit.[85]

In the story of the good Samaritan,[86]
    those Jesus condemns—

the priest and the Levite—
are the very ones who didn't do anything.
They surely didn't do anything wrong:
they didn't rough their neighbor
or knock him down;
they didn't take what little the robbers'd left,
though this was a fine opportunity;
they didn't even lecture him on his imprudence,
ranting, "It's no wonder!
We told you so, didn't we?"
No, they just left him alone.
We can't even say they let him fall:
they merely left him where he'd already fallen.
That's all.
To tell the truth, they didn't know this man.
They'd sinned against the Holy Spirit—only.
Then there's Dives.[87]
He didn't walk all over Lazarus,
fleece or exploit him.
He didn't even sermonize,
"Naturally, you haven't got a cent—
lazy and wild and improvident as you are!"
He simply didn't see Lazarus.

That's our problem, too: we don't see.
We don't see the misery on earth;
we don't see those two men out of every three in the world
who are starving.
We'd have to stir ourselves a bit
to see their anguish,
their distress;

to see the eyes
                        they haven't the strength to focus on us,
            the eyes
                        they have no reason to focus on us.
After all, what good would it do them?
    They've been with us so long
            and we haven't seen them yet.
        "Philip, after all this time . . ."[38]
We'd have to remind ourselves
    that we belong to the same community as they.
        Now, the only community big enough for Christ
                    is mankind.
God came to save all men.
        He told us so:
            "I have other sheep, too,
                    that aren't in this fold;
                and I have to go find them."[39]
But how can He go
        if we refuse to?
He's counting on us.
        "Listen, now. I'm sending you . . ."[40]
And what do we do?
    We stay in our little sphere—to preserve our virtue
                (like the man with only one talent).
        "This environment's good for me, so I never leave it.
            What a blessing!
        One mustn't waste the opportunities God gives."
Still, if we never "go out" of our milieu,
        both we and it have ceased to be Christian,
            though we may not be aware of the fact.
A "Catholic circle" is a contradiction in terms.

"Hermetic," "sheltered" surroundings are places
where the Holy Spirit's been made sterile.
He's a creator, not a conservator.
"Come, creative Spirit!"[41]

The episode of Cornelius the centurion illustrates
how horrified the smug can be
when they find that the Spirit's been given to "pagans"
as well as them.
"The Holy Spirit descended on all
as they listened to Peter's message.
The believers with a Judaic background were astonished
that the gift of the Spirit was bestowed on the heathen,
who were speaking different languages
and glorifying God.
Peter settled the problem by asking,
'Can anyone refuse these people the water of baptism,
since they've received the Holy Spirit
just as we did?' "[42]

Perhaps we, too, had better examine the "paganism"
of some of our brothers outside the fold.
We may discover that it contains surer tokens
of the Spirit of sharing
and mutual understanding
("they were speaking different languages")
than we'll ever detect in the conservative sectarianism
of some within.

All those Christ spoke to after His Resurrection
were sent forth,

oriented outward,
propelled toward others.

To Mary Magdalene He said,
"Go to My disciples and tell them . . ."[43]

To Peter,
"Feed My lambs."[44]

And to all,
"Go and teach . . ."[45]
"As the Father has sent Me, so I send you."[46]

Of the two men from Emmaus we read,
"Getting up immediately,
they returned to Jerusalem
and related what'd happened."[47]

"But," we may object, "I couldn't do that.
I haven't got what it takes.
What could I possibly give the poor?"
(That's what the man with a single talent said
as he buried it.)
"I'm no expert,
so how could I probe other people's problems?
I don't look around that much:
I'm more the quiet type,
and it always embarrasses me
to meddle in somebody else's business."
(Just like the priest and the Levite
who went ahead of the Samaritan.
They, too, were the soul of discretion.)

So we're tactful and well-bred,
deaf, dumb and blind?

That doesn't matter:
>> the Lord's cured many others before us!
>>> "The Holy Spirit will come
>>>> and teach you all things."[48]
>>> He'll change us—
>>>> if we want Him to,
>>>> if we welcome Him,
>>>> if we stop resisting Him
>>>>> ("Don't grieve the Holy Spirit"[49])
>>> and if we look to Him for everything.

If we're waiting for "something else,"
> we're waiting for the Antichrist.
>> Those who deem
>>> that love isn't what'll change the world
>>> and that there are better ways to achieve well-being—
>>>> they're the prophets of the Antichrist.
>> Those who are
>>> disappointed in the Holy Spirit,
>>> fed up trying to love their neighbor,
>>> tired of all this sharing,
>>>> all these paltry efforts to communicate,
>>>> these added problems
>>>>> that have to be solved
>>>>>> because we've bound ourselves up
>>>>>>> with others
>>>>>> in a chain of friendships,
>>>> all these complications,
>>>>> these frustrating failures,
>>>>> these wounds to endure and nurse;
>> those who refuse to go on loving,

suffering
and starting over endlessly,
beaten down
but "hoping against
hope"[50]—
they, too, are ready for an antichrist:
some snug little corner
where they'll be shielded
from these futile blows.

Sinning against the Holy Spirit means
preferring self-sufficiency,
isolating ourselves from this exhausting communion,
reaffirming our autonomy
and repelling the temptation
to start loving all over again
For God never stops tempting us:
He's always ambuscaded in our hearts.

Sinning against the Holy Spirit means
no longer believing He can change the world
because we no longer believe He can change us.
The genuine atheist isn't the man who declares,
"God doesn't exist,"
but the one who maintains that God can't remold him
and denies the Spirit's infinite power
to create,
transform
and raise him
from the dead.

He's the type who,

whether sixty years old or just fifteen,
goes around announcing,
"At my age, I can't change any more:
I'm too old, too weak, too far gone.
I've tried everything, and it hasn't worked.
No, there's nothing to be done for me!"

But with unflagging optimism, the Church sings each day,
"Send us Your Spirit,
and men will be created
and the face of the earth renewed!"[51]
The most potent creative force is the Holy Spirit.
His might reanimates the dead,
welds their parched bones together,
clothes them with flesh
and gives them vigor and life.
"Come, Creator!"

SEVEN: *LAY SPIRITUALITY*

How often have we been courageous enough to pray sincerely,
    "Come, Creator"?
How often have we really asked Him
    to create,
      re-create
      and reconstruct us,
      bring us down to death
          and back to life again?
Do we honestly want this consuming Spirit
   to destroy the awful power we have
     of resisting Him?

Telling Ananias about Saint Paul,
    who'd just been unhorsed by a voice from heaven,
   the Lord said,
      "I'll show him
        how much he has to suffer
          for My name's sake."[1]
The Spirit'd just overwhelmed Paul in an instant
     and at one stroke had smashed all his defenses.
   Who dares want that in his own life?
   Who's brave enough to desire,
         and so hasten,
            that revolutionizing
              presence?

Who's ready to plunge in
for the sheer fun of it?

Like all of us, the demoniac of Gerasa pleaded,
"Leave me alone, Jesus;
don't torture me!"[2]
"This man lived in the sepulchers"
(he frequented very proper places
and was well preserved).
"And no one could bind him any more—
not even with chains"
(he was perfectly independent,
autonomous,
unfettered);
"and though he'd often been bound"
(people'd tried to melt his heart
and get him to work with them;
and they'd almost won him over,
but he'd resisted with all his might),
"he'd rent the chains asunder
and broken the shackles to pieces,
and no one could master him"
(invulnerable and inaccessible among the tombs,
he was in full command of his domain
and ignored the rest of the world).
"Constantly, night and day"
(never missing one social gathering),
"he sauntered among the graves or on the mountains"
(the pinnacles of art!)
"shouting and howling"
(since that's the best way not to hear

what we don't want to hear,
and since we have to make our head swim
in order to forget)
"and gashing himself with stones"
(stones called nostalgia,
melancholy and vague yearnings,
the theater and heady novels—
as if he'd nothing to do but make himself suffer).
"When he saw Jesus from afar, he ran up to Him"
(a very clever boy,
he thought he'd forestall Christ
because it's always safer that way)
"and cried:
'Let me be, Jesus, Son of the most high God!'"
(in other words,
"Keep still!
Don't talk to me
about all those things,
all those people,
all that bliss
I don't give a hoot for,
those groups and teams
I hate,
those reunions and communions,
that solicitude and pity for others.
I've paid dearly for my freedom
and I intend to hold on to it,
so don't come bothering me with all that stuff").

"But Jesus commanded, 'Unclean spirit, get out of this man!'
Then He asked, 'What's your name?'

and was told, 'My name is Legion,
for there are many of us.'"

(If there were so many then, what must it be now!)

We all know the rest of the story.
Unable to escape Jesus' power,
the devils asked to be sent into a nearby herd of swine,
thinking that there, at least,
this persistent God would leave them
undisturbed.
He let them go,
and the herd—
some two thousand of them—
stampeded down the hillside
and drowned in the sea.
The townsmen ran out to learn what'd happened
and, when they came to Jesus,
they saw the demoniac sitting down,
dressed
and in his right mind.
(He'd certainly given up everything
that makes a party delightful.
Imagine: sitting down,
dressed
and in his right mind—
what austerity!)
Panic struck them;
they thought,
"Suppose things like this started happening regularly—
why, life'd become unlivable,"
and they entreated Jesus to leave their country.

As Christ was climbing into the boat,
        the former demoniac begged permission
                to stay with Him;
    but Jesus refused and said,
        "Go back home
            to your family
                and tell them everything the Lord's done
                        for you
                    in His mercy."

The ex-demoniac'd made a good retreat.
    He felt truly changed,
                liberated from his devils
                and ready for holiness.
    The only logical conclusion seemed to be
        to enter a monastery
        or,
            if he couldn't—
                    "my ailing mother, you know,"
                    "my husband and my children"—
    well, then, be patient
                and live in the world physically
                    while keeping his heart in the cloister,
                        his soul at the altar
                        and his eyes on heaven.

"Go back home
        to your family,"
                Jesus told him.
    "As a layman, you've got a different job to do
                and you have to serve Me elsewhere.

Work for others;
    talk to them about Me,
    tell the world how merciful I am,
            instead of daydreaming about this boat
                that isn't meant for you.
And don't think of your life as a poor second choice:
    it's a beautiful life,
            and you can use it to satisfy all those people
                who need to have you show them
                    'what the Lord's done'
                    and what His love can accomplish."

Just like him, we have to return to our own life—
    that "stupid" life
            we're so dissatisfied with,
    that "stupid" life
            we've always failed to consider sacred,
    that "stupid" life
            where God's been waiting to meet us
                right along,
                though we never realized it.

"Lay spirituality" should consist in believing
            in the sacred worth
of what people call their "profane" life.

What most of us lack is pride and joy:
                    the thrilling awareness
                        that we have a mission
                        and that we're serving God

wherever we are
from morning till night.

We're not indolent;
we work courageously,
desperately
and, often, excessively—
but without gladness.
Swamped by some occupation we deem purely secular,
we try to excuse the shameful paganism of it
by sporadic attempts at prayer and recollection.
We know we can't just chuck the whole thing,
so we cut corners here and there
and whittle it down as much as possible.

That's why all our "religion" has so little bearing
on our life—
our work,
our weariness,
our cares
and our sufferings.
Oh, yes, we all admit the "religious life" is preferable
("Mary's chosen the best way"[3]),
but we insist it isn't for us.
"When I was young, I dreamt of becoming a nun.
Well, maybe later when I'm a widow . . ."
"I have too much to do, right now;
but someday, when I've retired,
I'll start praying and meditating again."

As soon as a layman's faith grows a bit stronger,
he starts yearning for the monastic life,

> envying, imitating religious
> and waiting for the day
>> when he can practice this religion
>> of widowers and pensioners
>>> in peace and pious leisure.

Religious themselves are often chiefly responsible
> for such dispirited inertia.
Many of them think the lay state's like their own—
> but debased;
> so they find it quite natural that,
>> as soon as a layman shows some progress
>> in the spiritual life,
> he should start doing what they do.
When a lawyer asked Saint Catherine of Siena
> to become his spiritual director,
> she answered, "Yes, I will—
>> provided, first, that you leave your wife
>> and, secondly, that you abandon your profession."
The implication was:
> "Only then can you hope to become a saint."
Few laymen dare see it differently
> and, as a result,
> they renounce holiness for the time being.

Lay persons, by and large, underestimate their vocation.
> They don't understand
>> that God needs them
>>> right where they are
>>> to carry on His work among men,
>> that He's counting on them

to perfect and sanctify the world;
they don't realize
that He's committed this task,
this business,
these children,
this man and this woman
to *them,*
and that we're all like the wise and
prudent manager
who's been put in charge
of some of his Master's goods
and servants
in order to give each one what he needs
when he needs it.[4]

Let's look at it this way:
God needed someone,
where we are now,
to guide this child,
to comfort this man or woman,
to perform this job,
to prove His love.
Couldn't He have done that Himself, without relying on us?
(In *Quo Vadis*, for instance,
when Saint Peter's had his fill
and decides to go away, to desert,
Christ takes his place, declaring,
"I'm going to Rome to be crucified again.")
Yes, God could've done everything all by Himself,
but He so made the world
that things wouldn't be as good that way.

[207]

He's chosen to need men;
He's willed that we be necessary to Him
      for the fulfillment of His designs.
              "You'll do greater deeds than I."[5]
He's permanently set up the universe in such a way
      that God with man can accomplish more
            than God alone.
He became flesh
      and forever bound Himself to being incarnate.
             "As the Father has sent Me,
                so now I send you."[6]

He has sent us;
      and if we don't live up to His expectations,
            our mission'll be a failure.
Naturally, He didn't ask how we felt about it.
      No, He loves and trusts us too much for that.
          He knew full well we'd stagger with dread
             if He asked us what we thought.
So He simply decided,
      "I'm going to send him.
          He'll make out well. . . .
          This woman'll be so happy later on. . . .
          And these people will eventually be glad
             to co-operate with Me.
          I'll be with them
             ('He's going ahead of you into Galilee''),
          and someday they'll rejoice with Me."

He's relying on us:
      He's entrusted His work to us

and He's waiting for us to do it.
He needs us
    to make this man or woman happy,
    to do this particular task,
    to manifest His tenderness and His fidelity,
        His joy and goodness,
          His patience and trust and courage.
If only we realized that!
If only we took a little more pride in it
    and felt that,
        wherever we are,
    we're God's lieutenants.
The word *lieutenant* means "one who takes
        another's place,"
    and it suggests
        that we have to take God's place
          with regard to those He's confided to us,
        that we have to substitute for Him
          and, in His stead, do the job
            He's left in *our* hands.

Since the Incarnation, our Lord has only one desire:
    to recommence the human life
        which He loved so fondly
        and in which He healed and cured,
          instructed,
          elevated and purified souls
            so effectively,
          served His Father
            so faithfully
          and loved both God and man

so well.

That's why He wants additional human natures:

people who'll let Him start all over again.

And He needs us to do that.

Thirty-three years wasn't long enough

to do and show all He meant to.

As Claudel says,

"Have pity on Him,

for all He had was thirty-three years to suffer."

A man can die only once.

Christ needed to suffer and love in every possible way.

But He couldn't love like a woman or a mother

and He couldn't die the death of an old man;

and unless we let Him,

many of the things He wished to do

will have to go undone

and some of the homage

He wanted to offer His Father

will be lost.

God must be adored and glorified,

no matter how lowly our calling.

If His Son spent thirty years

sawing and planing

and helping around the house;

if Mary spent thirty years

(and many more after)

performing the same round of duties:

cooking and praying,

washing and cleaning;

if God desired that cult,

that liturgy,
that office
("I'm reciting my office"),
we shouldn't look for a way out
but, rather, be only too glad and proud
that we've been chosen to keep doing that for Him.

In every day's Preface we repeat,
"It's indeed fitting and right,
proper and salutary,
that we thank You
always
and everywhere . . ."
Then we return to our "stupid life,"
which seems empty;
our "stupid job,"
which seems meaningless;
our "stupid home"
and our "stupid family."
And yet is there a single place
or a single moment
when God doesn't need to be adored and glorified?
Isn't it "fitting and right,
proper and salutary,"
to give thanks right where we are?
Perhaps we're here for the sole reason
that no one's ever yet offered thanks or adoration
in this spot.
We must sanctify everything
and adore everywhere,
at all times

and in all places.
That's the sum total of what Christ did for thirty years.

Seeing that God's Son was sent into the world
("God loved the world so much
that He delegated His only Son to redeem it"[8]),
shouldn't we be delighted
to set out each morning,
to be sent into the world?
Shouldn't we be overjoyed to hear Him say
"You're so truly My sons and daughters
and I'm so pleased with you
that I'm sending you forth
to save the world"?
That's our job,
our mission—
in the world.
"Father, don't take them out of the world."[9]

"It's impossible," we maintain.
"Since I have to believe God loves me,
I can't think He put me here deliberately—
here, in this barren desert,
in this hopeless situation,
amid failure
and incomprehensible,
exhausting,
needless suffering."
And what about the One in whom He was *perfectly* pleased?[10]
Where did the Father let Him go?
To Gethsemane,

to the Praetorium,
to the Cross,
    where He was nailed in anguish,
        dereliction
        and infamy.

"God didn't spare His own Son."[11]
    And it's because He loves us
        that He doesn't spare us, either.
We should shout for joy at being so honored,
    for we could never've dared hope
        for such close brotherhood with Christ.

And just as God resurrected Him,
    so He'll resurrect us, too—
        on the third day.

Meanwhile, we have to work.
    "My Father works constantly,
        and so do I."[12]
    "So that the world may know
        that I love the Father
            and do as He's commanded Me,
    let's get up and go from here."[13]
        In other words,
            let's leave our seclusion
            and get busy.

Remarrying our husband or wife,
rebegetting our children,
reassuming our family and professional duties—
        that's the essence of our religious life.

We needn't look at God furtively
    while tending to the souls He's committed to us,
    since we're never nearer to Him
        than when we love them
           as He bids us.

Instead of turning away from them
    we should look at them more closely.
Christ's in them
    and is waiting to be discovered
      so He may grow.
At the same time,
    He's in us
      so we may love them.
We need all the love God pours into our heart
    if we're to love,
      as we should
      and as they require,
    husband and wife,
    child and neighbor.
We're so short on love
    that even the Incarnation isn't too much to fill us.
If the Word keeps becoming flesh in us, day after day,
    we can be sure
He's aiming at another life beyond ours—
      some individual,
      some family
        that He wants to imbue with love
          and transfigure.

What we're worth spiritually

has nothing to do with how often we receive
                    or how long we pray.
We must eat to live,
            not live to eat.
For that reason, we should center our lives in charity,
                    and not in the virtue of religion.
        Our surest declaration of faith
            consists in what we've accomplished
                in our profession
                and in our family.

We're discouraged because we don't know what our mission is.
So many good Christians've been trying for years
                to pray ten minutes a day,
                    but all to no avail.
The reason is
        that their work and their prayer aren't homogeneous.
They pray without working
            and work without praying,
                    but put the two side by side
                        like airtight compartments.
They never come to understand
            baptism gave them a missionary vocation
                that's far more important
                    than the "religious vocation."
They lack faith in their calling as Christians.
        "Blessed be God, the Father of
                        our Lord Jesus Christ,
            who . . . chose us in Him,
                    before the foundation of the world . . .
                to manifest the splendor of His grace."[14]

We can't, for a fact, think more highly of God
                than we do of our life;
we can't love Him any more
                than we love His will;
our professional frame of mind
                reveals our true religious attitude.
    The big obstacle to sanctity
            is that we're blind to our mission:
    we don't realize
                that our life stopped being profane
                    the minute we were baptized
                and that it became a cult,
                        a liturgy,
                        an office,
                        an apostolate.

What matters is,
        not the kind of mission we have,
        but awareness that we do have one
                and the unwavering conviction that God's with us,
                        that He's sent us—
                            wherever we are.

    People who imagine
        they've chosen their own lives
            are lonesome,
                isolated
                and melancholy;
whereas those who know
        God's made the choice for them
            and has assigned what they must do each day—
they abide in God,
        just as the Son,

who was sent into the world,
remained united to the Father:
"He never abandons Me,
because I always do what pleases Him."[15]
"The very works
that My Father's given Me to accomplish
and that I carry out
bear witness to Me that He's sent Me."[16]

"If you keep My commandments,
you'll abide in My love,
as I've kept My Father's commandments
and abide in His love.
I've told you these things
so that My joy could be in you
and make yours complete."[17]
As long as we consider our activities
from a purely human standpoint,
they'll keep tossing us back and forth
between the most naïve zeal
and the bitterest repugnance.
But Jesus came to tell us "these things"
so that His joy and peace might permeate all we do
and give it unity.
Once we're convinced
we can make one of God's dreams and
desires come true,
our "stupid existence" will glow with pride,
gratitude
and bliss.

"*Ite, missa est*" doesn't just mean
       "Mass is over. You may leave."
  It means
       "Go, now!
           You're being com*missioned;*
              this is your *send-off.*"
     (If we were merely being dis*missed*
                  and *sent back* home,
       it'd be rather indelicate of us to answer,
             "Thanks be to God!")
    "*Ite, missa est*" means
       "Go, now!
       Go spread the Good News;
          go broadcast it;
          go tell and explain it to everybody.
       Go rekindle ice-bound hearts;
          go heal the wounded;
          go make fallow ground fertile.
       Go bring comfort and light;
          go unseal springs of living water."

"The Word became flesh."
    That's the last thing the Church tells us
         after our send-off,
       as if to remind us that that flesh is now ourselves—
          "sent into the world."

The end of each day's Mass
    should thrust us into the world
        like a new Pentecost.

EIGHT: *THE LORD'S HANDMAID*

The first Pentecost,
the first mission in the Spirit
proposed and agreed to,
the first acquiescence
total enough for the Word to become flesh,
for the Incarnation to take place
and for God to be "brought into
the world,"
was the Annunciation.

Mary's the one who gave herself up entirely,
who surrendered,
body and soul,
to this invasion by the Spirit.
"And the Word became flesh"[1]
and could start living among us.

Mary believed in her vocation
("Here I am—the Lord's handmaid"[2])
and gave herself to it
immediately
and with every fiber of her being
("Let what You've said be done in me").
She didn't ask herself
whether or not her lowly existence was compatible

with the announcement just made to her.
Without even thinking of herself,
she trusted in God
and said "Yes."

She leaped for joy because of God her Saviour.
She recognized Him
and believed it was He.
She believed, too, that He needed her,
that He needed a mother,
a daughter
who was faithful enough
to become His mother.
She believed
and promptly set out.
"The angel left,
and Mary arose and went with haste . . ."*

What's especially remarkable about the Blessed Virgin
is her faith.
She lived a life of faith—
exactly like us.
We mustn't ever think of her
as some unapproachable queen
to be admired from afar,
but, rather, as an example for every day
to be imitated in our lives.
("That man is you.
That woman is you.")
The worst part about overstressing
the exceptional aspects of Mary

is that we feel excused,
at once and for always,
from copying her.

"Oh! come, now," we argue, "she had the
unparalleled privilege
of being conceived immaculate."
Let's think for a minute:
what, precisely, does that mean?
It means she was conceived already baptized
and, as a result, had grace
from the first instant of her conception.
We received grace a few days after our birth.
She never had original sin.
We no longer have it.
"Yes, but she had all kinds of other privileges besides!"
Like what?
Was she exempt from death?
No.
From suffering?
No.
From concupiscence?
Yes;
but so was Adam,
and that didn't keep him from falling.

The most extraordinary thing in Mary's life is her faith,
and meditating on it
fills us with endless rapture and amazement.
To get a clearer idea of it,
we should compare it with the faith of other saints—

Joan of Arc, for instance.
Now, there's a similar case:
a sixteen-year-old girl,
an angel and some saints
and a mission.
Yet, even with a well-defined and purely
temporal mission
like saving France,
she had to be told over and over for three years
before she could start believing in it;
she had to let the idea sink in
and get used to it slowly.

Mary was sixteen, too,
busy with household chores
and engaged to a craftsman,
when an angel appeared to her
and announced a whole series of things
that were much harder to believe:
she'd be a mother
and remain a virgin;
she'd bear a son—
a saviour
who'd redeem
the world,
an incomparable
being
who'd rule eternally.

Mary's reaction to this speech revealed a humility

that was infinitely truer
than anything we could ever've imagined.
We think we're humbler than she
because we realize we're sinners;
still, the very fact that we're sinners
is precisely what keeps us from being humble.
Humility consists in knowing the distance—
the infinite distance—
between God and ourselves.
The Blessed Virgin had a very accurate
notion of Him
and, so, was infinitely humble.
Admitting that we're sinners, on the other hand,
means knowing only the distance—
the altogether finite distance—
between a sinless creature
and a sinful one.
Furthermore (and this is the whole point),
our sins screen God from us,
depriving us of Him
and blinding us where He's concerned.
Compared to us, Mary was perfectly humble;
and that's why she raised no questions.
We would've gasped,
"Can't be! That'll never work!
I don't feel I'm ready yet.
Wait just a little—
say, two or three more retreats—
till I put on the finishing touches."
Mary didn't do that.
In all simplicity, she thought,

"God's great enough and good enough,
                generous and powerful enough
        to accomplish such things
                in His poor handmaid.
    In a word, He's God,
                and, so, I'm not surprised."
Knowing only ourselves,
        we'd have concluded He couldn't do anything
                with us;
    but, knowing God,
        she was sure He could do anything He wanted.
Hence, Mary acquiesced, once and for all,
                and said, "Do with me as You wish."
Her fiat was the fiat of Gethsemane—the very same:
                "Not My will, but Yours"[4];
        the fiat we'll repeat in the Our Father
                when we're a bit more like her:
                "May Your will be done!"
    We're all required to reach the level
                where we can say,
                "Do what You want with me."

Mary consented to let God take over her life;
    and, as always, He set to work immediately.
        (With God,
                things start happening
                the minute we say "Please" or "So be it.")
    No sooner had she agreed
                than she began to be humiliated,
                                perplexed
                                and thwarted;

right from the first,
she began to suffer.

How did she know it was God?
The way we all do:
by His demands.
A very exacting child,
He asked for everything
and led her to sacrifice it so completely
that she realized
only God could require that much.
Her deep-seated attitude toward God found scope
in her Son.
The more He wanted, the more she understood
He was God;
and she kept repeating,
"I'm Your servant, Lord.
May what You've said be done in me."

Everything started to go wrong from the beginning,
even before Jesus' birth.
First of all, she had to sacrifice her fiancé.
When we read the Gospels,
we know the story'll come out all right—
like in those novels we've read over and over;
but when this was actually happening,
it wasn't quite that simple.
Mary and Joseph loved each other—very much so,
but she didn't think she had a right
to divulge God's secret.
We see that throughout her life:

she always felt she shouldn't interfere
or rush God's plans
but, rather, trust
and wait.
So, like Saint John the Baptist,
she let herself be imprisoned in solitude,
immured in mystery.
And this went on for days and days.
It's easy to imagine the humiliations,
the anguish
and the problems
Mary faced at every turn.
All this time, Joseph was wonderful.
Of course, they were in love. . . .
Thank goodness they were,
for it's only loving each other
as much as they did
and the way they did
that enabled them to weather that storm.
It seems to me that Joseph learned to believe in God
because he believed in Mary.
Never once did he doubt her
or think of himself;
but, sensing something inscrutable
and not wishing to meddle in it,
he drew aside and waited in the shadows.
Poor Joseph!
God had stepped into his life, too,
and, as He always does, had begun by crossing him.
Abraham and Zacharias, for example,
wanted a child;

and, naturally, they didn't have one.
As for Joseph, well, he just had to accept everything.
And we have proof that he did accept it well—
decisive proof, I'd say, that he reached a state
of total respect,
compliance
and docility
to the workings of God.
The sign?
The fact that he slept!
(Remember Saint Peter?)
An angel had to wake Joseph from sleep.
There was the high point of his spiritual life;
it meant that, at some moment,
he'd conquered and understood.
As I said before,
he believed in Mary so deeply
that he owed his cure to her.
His faith in her brought out
and strengthened his faith
in God.
Because he loved and trusted her so much,
he learned to believe
that all was well,
that all that comes from God is good.
Then, later—much later,
an angel arrived to explain everything to him.
Mary'd waited
till God chose to reveal His secrets.

If only we were as patient!

For that's the only way God can further His plans in us.
> Mary, in her perfect patience, always seconded them;
> but we always want to hurry things up
>> and act on our own.

Let's recall the story of Sara.[5]
> God had promised her a son;
>> but, as usual, He was moving pretty slowly.
> When she'd waited long enough,
>> she said to herself,
>>> "I'm going to take matters into my own hands
>>>> and do this myself, instead of God.
>>> He's a little sluggish, kind of snail-paced.
>>> Just leave it to me:
>>>> I know what to do."

She did.
> She got involved in that business with Agar.
>> Sure she'd found a way to make Abraham a father,
>>> she gave him Agar as his mate.

The rest of the story's only too well known:
> squabbles between the two women,
> scuffles between the two sons,
>> Ismael against Isaac
>> and Agar against Sara,
> and, finally, disappointment,
>> heartbreak
>>> and bitterness for everyone.

Man'd interfered with God's designs;
> lacking faith and patience,
> he'd decided to do things his own way.
Mary, on the other hand, said,
>> "May Your will be done in me,"

and she let it be done.
"Work in me
and make me allow You to work."

For so many of us,
religion's a way of intruding at the wrong time,
trying to stir up God,
bustling about
in a place of our own choosing
instead of the one where God asks us
to render Him service,
homage
and thanks.
The Incarnation is Jesus entering into our life,
Jesus consecrating the life we live.
Imagine: thirty years in the house,
thirty years without going anywhere,
thirty years without seeing anyone.
Well, that was our Saviour's life—
duller,
more monotonous
and, seemingly, less useful
than any of us leads.
And it was the same with Mary.
She spent thirty years wondering
why she'd had to let the Lord enter into her life
in so extraordinary and difficult a way
only to live such a banal,
apparently wasted
existence.
But she remembered all these things

and pondered them in her heart.[6]
She passed her whole life
repeating a single statement God had made
(". . . one word,
and my soul will be healed . . ."[7]);
and the Holy Spirit—
the best of teachers—
kept reiterating everything the angel'd told her.

One thing we can be sure of:
we never understand an utterance of God's
on the first try.
It has to germinate in us very slowly;
and, every time circumstances change,
we discover some new meaning in it.
Mary believed in a single word God had spoken
and she repeated it to herself
her whole life through.
Do we do that?
Which of His sayings do we repeat?
What encounters with Him do we remember?
What expressions of His have we found so nourishing
and healing
that we carry them with us
as food for the journey,
as viaticum?
Still, that's what we're all asked to do:
to believe perseveringly
in the dark
in something we once saw
in the light,

to believe steadfastly
in something that once appeared evident
in joy.

Mary's fidelity was put to a stiff test right from the start.
Her baby was born in loneliness
and destitution;
she'd never been poorer,
never more tired
or solitary.
Yet it was the Lord Himself
who'd chosen the hour of His birth—
exactly the wrong time,
exactly the one moment we'd have
ruled out.

Then there was the massacre of the Holy Innocents.
Do we appreciate the scandal that caused?
The first effect of the Saviour's birth was that
each family in the area was plunged into mourning;
every tiny babe under two was murdered, butchered,
and all the other mothers—
in their motherhood, they were
Mary's sisters,
and she knew what it meant to be
a mother—
suddenly found themselves left with nothing.
Can we honestly think
her heart didn't burst with sorrow for them?
What excruciating agony
and desolate darkness

her faith must've gone through;
and what a superhuman effort it must've taken
for her to remain loyal,
to believe,
repeat
and even remember
the words of the *Magnificat:*
"His mercy extends from one generation
to another.
He exalts the lowly
and fills the hungry with good things.
Mindful of His love,
He protects Israel, His servant."[8]
(Really, now!
If that were so,
how could He let
those infants be slaughtered
and those families
ripped apart?)
To us, it all seems perfectly simple,
perfectly normal.
We've even made a feast out of it;
but when it happened, it was no feast.

We'd all like to do great things.
Mary, however, was satisfied to let God do them in her.
He did—
through the grief and the suffering of
His handmaid;
and she remained unshaken,
sure that all was right

and that the Lord knew what
He was doing
better than she.
She kept saying,
"Just as high as the heavens are above the earth,
so are His ways above our ways
and His thoughts above our thoughts."[9]

Thirty years went by like that—
thirty years in which not another thing occurred,
thirty years of faith and self-conquest,
thirty years during which she must've wondered
why all was at a standstill
and whether anything was going to happen.
According to Mauriac in his beautiful *Vie de Jésus*,
the Blessed Virgin never forgot
the sharp point of the sword Simeon'd talked about,
and at certain moments she asked herself
whether the suffering he'd foretold
didn't consist in always being the sole witness
of this immense love.
God was living there,
and she was the only one to watch with Him,
the only one to serve as
a sanctuary lamp.

Yet she didn't say anything or run to tell the neighbors
She held her tongue and believed—
believed Jesus could save the world
while He remained silent,
as the Apostles should've believed

[235]

                        He could save them
                    while He slept.
Constant,
    she didn't make a single mistake the others made;
    she held fast,
        believed,
        and stayed in her prison—
                the prison of faith.

And what's more (for it's not enough to acquiesce),
        she continued to hope.
    We have to hope against all hope;
    we have to trust that what we call failure
            is really a sign of the mysterious victories
                God's love'll carry off.
Resignation's never the same as faith.
    Zacharias, for instance, had resigned himself
                to being childless,
                and we know what happened to him.[10]
    He was supposed to look to God for everything
                till the very end of his life.
Genuine confidence doesn't say,
            "Oh, well! Too bad this won't work out,
                but I'm reconciled to the idea."
    Instead of that, it maintains,
            "What seems a poor shot still hits the bull's-eye.
            Things look as if they won't come off
                and, somehow, they do—
                    in another way,
                    by other means.
        I don't understand how or why

and I'm not supposed to,
but I take the Lord's word for it."

In prison, John kept repeating,
"The deaf hear,
the blind see,
the lame dance
and lepers are evangelized. . . ."[11]
And in Nazareth, where Jesus lived silently,
Mary re-echoed, day after day,
"He'll be great.
He'll be the Saviour,
and His kingdom'll last forever.
Nothing's impossible for God."[12]

After Jesus'd turned twelve,
as the Gospels relate,
He very tersely told His parents
He had to tend to His Father's business.[13]
They didn't understand what He meant,
but Mary understood
that she didn't understand
and she was willing to have it that way.
When it comes to faith, hope and trust,
God makes appalling demands,
and His saints are people who've made up their mind
to believe without understanding.
Charles de Foucauld used to say,
"I've got to cling to faith for dear life;
and I don't even know whether God loves me,

for He never tells me so."
With souls like Mary and Charles de Foucauld,
He never does—not any more;
but with us,
He will yet—now and then.

If we've ever meditated on this incident in the Temple,[16]
we should've been properly shocked
at the way Jesus answered His father
and His mother.
A mere slip of a boy,
He'd stayed away from His parents for three days,
and when His mother found Him and gently asked,
"My son, why did You do that to us?
Your father and I have been looking for You,
just heartsick with worry!"
He replied,
"Why were you looking for Me?
Didn't you know . . .?"
We feel He could surely have found something else to say,
but that's because we don't know a thing about it.
Jesus was twelve,
and this was His first pilgrimage to the Temple
since the day He'd been circumcised.
Around the holidays, at that time,
Jerusalem was the scene of delirious excitement;
trumpets resounded in the distance,
and singing crowds came to pray.
Jesus entered into the Temple—
a place where God was loved,
where everything reminded Him of

His Father,
where all was associated
with worship and liturgy,
adoration, thanksgiving
and sacrifice,
and where,
for the first time in His life,
He felt happy
and at home.
So He stayed there,
raised above Himself,
lost in wonder,
oblivious of everything;
and, though all the others left, He remained behind.
When His parents came searching for Him three days later,
He spoke like someone waking from a dream:
"You mean you left?
How could you?
And why did you have to hunt for Me?
Surely, you didn't think
I'd be anywhere but in My Father's house!"

Perhaps the very same thing happened to us
one Sunday morning.
We'd all gone to Mass together—the whole family;
and one of the children stayed in his pew
for a little extra thanksgiving.
After we'd been home a few hours,
we started wondering where he was
and checking all the possibilities:
"Oh, he must be having another gabfest

or he's playing over at his friend's
or . . ."
Another two hours,
and we all became nervous and apprehensive
and started looking everywhere,
till someone finally suggested,
"You know,
he's kind of a funny kid
Suppose we try the church . . ."
And that's just where we found him.
To our remonstrance
"So this is where you were!
Why didn't you tell us you wanted to stay after?'
he answered,
"Oh! you left?
How could you do that?
Don't you like it here?
Aren't you glad to be with our Father?
What made you think I'd be elsewhere?
Didn't you realize I'd be in my Father's house?
It's such a good place to be!"
But we stood there,
gaping
and dumbfounded,
and didn't understand.

The beginning'd been bad enough for Mary and Joseph;
but when Jesus began His public life,
things were worse still.
The harshest words of His ever recorded in Scripture
were all spoken to His mother.

At Cana, He told her,
"Woman, let Me alone.
My hour hasn't come yet."[15]
Another time, somebody whispered,
"Your mother and Your relatives are outside
and want to see You."[16]
You'd think He'd get up;
but, no, He looked at those He was talking to
and said,
"Whoever listens to God's word—
he's My father and My mother and My sisters."
Now, it must surely hurt a mother to hear that sort of thing.
We wouldn't have the heart to talk to ours like that.
But Mary could take it:
that's how she served God.
The others lit up and gave themselves airs:
"Yes, indeed!
I'm His real father and mother,
His real brother and sister!"
And the poor Blessed Virgin stood in the background
thinking,
"That's the way He wants it.
I mustn't say anything
but just go along with Him."

Women in the different towns used to exclaim,
"How lucky the mother who carried
and nursed You!"[17]
But they were completely wrong.
Physical relationship means nothing;
neither does motherhood in the flesh.

We needn't envy the people who lived in Christ's day:
those who listen to the word of God
and follow it
and believe—
they're the fortunate ones.
Mary alone truly understood what Jesus'd said;
she alone'd been tasting that bliss for years now.
Her faithfulness,
she knew subconsciously,
was uniting her very closely to her Son
and preparing the way for total communion.
The more He took from her,
the freer she became.
He's the one who taught her, beforehand,
to climb every last inch of Calvary;
He's the one who helped purify her motherhood
of all that was too human,
too natural
and,
therefore
and in spite of herself,
somewhat possessive
and exclusive.
By detaching her from everything,
He made her worthy of Himself.

Jesus kept His hardest sayings for Mary
because He knew she'd co-operate
better than anyone else would
and because He wanted her to resemble Him
more than anyone else did.

As for her, she was well aware
  that His words and exigencies were just
              the outward proof
      of the deep accord between them.
Young though she was,
  Mary learned what it means to obey
          and,
          rising above her affliction,
      thanked God for what caused it:
          that nearness,
              resemblance
              and union
                  He was achieving in her heart.
Never once was she scandalized,
  but always bowed to His will
          and told herself He was right.
That's how the Lord made her more like Himself
          in her detachment and purity of purpose;
and that's why,
              on Calvary,
      she emerged from her silence,
          the only creature worthy of standing
              near Him.

Yes, on Calvary—she was there.
          "Blessed are those who listen to God's word
              and act upon it."[18]
But where were the rest—
  all the "brothers" and "sisters" of a few months ago,
  those who'd puffed themselves up
          as they listened to God's word?

They'd all disappeared,
    every last one of them.
She was there alone—
        she who'd agonized because of that word,
        she whose heart'd been pierced by it.
It's always like that:
        the only ones who remember God's word
            are those who first suffer from it;
        it bears fruit in them
            since they're the only ones it's actually reached.
Mary had grasped the lesson:
        it's not the mother or the sister who are fortunate,
            but the soul that listens and practices,
                believes and remains firm.
That's why she was there on Calvary.

Even though she didn't understand,
    she must've repeated the fiat of that first moment
        incessantly;
    she must've fastened on to the fiat
        that'd sprung from her fidelity
        and sealed her vocation.
She was caught up, we have to realize,
        in an incomprehensible mystery,
        in a sort of apparent opposition
            between the two beings she loved most—
                the Father
                and the Son.
The cry of Jesus,
            "My God, My God, why have You
                abandoned Me?"[19]

wrenched the very sinews of her faith and hope;
and yet,
         deep in her loyal heart,
      she believed that everything was right and good,
                  that it had to happen that way,
                  that God knew what He was doing.

Unable to fathom what was going on,
      she still assented,
               adhered
               and lent herself to it all.
She was there to make the supreme sacrifice
               and breathe another fiat.
It was no longer enough to say,
      "Lord, here I am—Your handmaid"
            (that was relatively easy);
this time, she had to say,
      "Lord, here is my son—Your servant.
         Do what You want with Him."
There'd been a first fiat in her life,
      but it's this last one that really counted.
She truly became a mother on Calvary
      because the only way to become a mother,
            in the full sense of the word,
      is to give everything:
            give life
            and then concur with all the thoughts
                        and desires
                     and the whole mission
                        of one's child.

      On Calvary,

Mary brought forth Jesus in His Redemption—
that is, in His work,
in His specific mission.
She gave her consent and became wholly a mother.
That sums up the life of the creature
who drew closest to God.

We, too, want to draw close to Him;
but would we have recognized Him
in that kind of existence,
in such a poor,
topsy-turvy,
dismal,
frustrating life?
We often sigh, "If only I'd lived Mary's life!"
The truth is we *have* lived it,
for each and every one of us is God's servant,
in whom He hopes to do great things.

The deadliest mistake in our attitude toward Mary
would be to place her on such a high pedestal
that she'd no longer have anything
in common with us.
If we admired her to the point of making
her unapproachable,
we'd nullify her message.
Mary's much more than a jewel of God's:
she's a mother,
our mother;
and what she wants is children

who are like her,
who are willing to be servants,
just as she was.

God wouldn't be a father if He didn't have sons and daughters.
He takes pride in having children—
children who bear fruit.[20]
From the moment He decided to be a father,
He made His whole glory consist in this.
that we start being sons and daughters
who resemble Him.
So, too, with Mary.
From the moment she agreed to be our mother,
her one desire, her one ambition,
was to have sons and daughters
like herself.
A mother's whole joy lies in having children
who mirror her.
When Saint Thérèse of the Child Jesus prayed to love God
as no one'd ever loved Him before,
I believe she was genuinely inspired
by the Blessed Virgin,
for if there's anything a mother dreams of
it's to see her children do even more
than she did.
That's all Mary desired,
all she prayed for.
Her Son died, promising us,
"You'll do greater deeds
than I've done."[21]
So how could she, His mother, wish otherwise?

Inseparable from all God wills, says and does,
>Mary can be defined as the servant of all His graces,
>>co-operating perfectly with His every plan.

That's how she operates in our life
>>>and exercises her motherhood.
>She doesn't want to reign over subjects:
>she wants to be surrounded by a throng of children
>>who are like her.

We must do God and Mary the honor of trusting in her enough
>to hope we'll come to resemble her.

Anything short of that'd be inexcusable,
>>tantamount to denying her motherhood.
For that's what we do in our specious humility:
>with our "Oh, I'm not worthy!"
>>and "I'll never make a go of it,"
>we put her in a corner,
>>solitary
>>and sterile.

But if she's a mother,
>then her whole joy consists in giving us life—
>>because that's the only joy mothers know.
And the patience they have!
>They love to teach,
>>love to educate.
Maybe we're afraid our sins'll dishearten Mary?
>No!
>>Mothers are tireless;
>>>and the more they can help and baby us,
>>>the more they like it.

It's the most difficult children
      who bring out all the mother in them,
   and the retarded
      who receive the greatest love.
No matter what mess we're in,
   Mary'll only want to help us that much more.

There's no use urging, "I don't have her privileges."
   Right, we don't;
      but she didn't have ours, either.
She carried our Lord for nine months;
   whereas we—
      we can communicate our whole life long,
         whenever we like.
There was no Communion for Mary.
She was immaculate, of course.
   Well, we're baptized;
      and each confession's another baptism
         that renews us.
Don't we believe in God's forgiveness?
Or perhaps we think
   He's stingy
      and gives as little grace as possible—
         a pinch here and a pinch there—
      so that Mary's the only one
         who got a good helping,
         because He was generous for once.

Every day, the Blessed Virgin had to invent a new fiat;
every day, she had to start afresh to discover God in her life
   in ways she hadn't at all foreseen.

[249]

That's precisely what we have to do.
　　We never recognize Him;
　　　　He always fools us,
　　　　and we're always scandalized.
"Blessed is she who has believed." [22]
　　Well, she who has believed is our mother;
　　　　and we'll have no peace,
　　　　　　　　no security,
　　　　　　till we follow her example
　　　　　　　　and accept her loving and constant invitation
　　　　　　　　　　to become like her,
　　　　　　　　　　to become her children.
　　Far from ever being sorry she's our mother,
　　　　she'll continually remind us
　　　　　　that *she* didn't always understand our Lord, either,
　　　　　　　　but always said "Yes,"
　　　　　　　　always agreed
　　　　　　　　and always marveled at Him.

For all eternity, she'll admire the great things God did
　　in His lowly handmaid. [23]
　　We, too, must be able to sing the *Magnificat* someday;
　　　　for only then shall we go to heaven—
　　　　　　when we finally let ourselves be astonished
　　　　　　　　by the wonders He'll have worked
　　　　　　　　in all His ignoble servants.

NINE: *HEAVEN*

Some people've never met God
        either in His written word
        or in forgiveness
        or in faith
          (which is superhuman)
        or in their neighbor
          (who's altogether too human)
        or in their lives
          (which are too worldly)
and yet fondly hope to meet Him
        in heaven.

We have to shatter this expectation,
        remedy this misconception,
before it leads to utter ruin.

If we haven't found God on earth,
        we won't find Him in heaven.
For heaven's not some other world
        where we go to escape;
the kingdom of heaven's already in us,[1]
        and we have to build it up with the graces God gives us.

God wants people who'll work with Him,
                not sit around and dream.[2]

If we're content to await the kingdom of God,
it'll never come.
His gifts in us are living
and efficacious;
they must produce results,
and they retain their true character as gifts
only if we give them to someone else in turn.

"This is eternal life:
knowing You,
the only true God,
and Him whom You've sent—
Jesus Christ."[8]
Those who haven't begun this eternal life on earth,
who haven't already been irradiated, here below,
by the presence and the love of God
(which are offered to every man
who comes into the world[4]),
and haven't found anything in their existence
to eternize—
those people will never get to heaven.

Earth is a place where we build our heaven.
God doesn't invite us to pass into the next world.
Rather, He's invited Himself into this world;
He's redeemed it
and released into it infinite forces
which He's entrusted to us
so we might transform it;
and, someday, He'll crown His work and ours
by making it eternal.

We're in this world forever,
>> so let's take it to heart and hurry to better it.
Heaven'll just be the stabilization
>>> and the full development
>> of what we'll have achieved
>>> with the gifts God gave us.
An "edifying" man isn't a pious mummer:
> he's a builder.

Too many Christians are spiritualists.
> They believe in the immortality of the soul
>>> but not in the resurrection of the flesh;
> they long to flee from this earth
>>> and cast off their bodies.
God, on the contrary, takes on a body
>>> and deems human flesh
>>>> a good conductor of divine power;
He reveals Himself through creation,
>> for the world, cast in His image, is God made visible;
He becomes incarnate
> and acquires a human nature;
He communicates His grace through the sacraments
> and will make all creation share
>>> in the glorious freedom of the sons of God.[5]
And it may well be that heavenly joy will consist,
>> not in having our human faculties suspended,
>> but in living our human life to the full,
>>> like the statue a sculptor carves
>>>> in accordance with his vision.
God'll have given Himself to us to such an extent
>> that He'll not only be contemplated in Himself

but also be reflected by the whole of creation.
The presence of the Giver won't make us scorn His gifts;
it'll shed brighter light on them.
We're not asked to choose between God and world,
but to discover Him in the world
and reveal Him to it.
Though we can't imagine or describe
what this face-to-face vision will be like,
its repercussions on man concern us even now.
The resurrection of the flesh teaches us
that our heavenly bliss will also be a human bliss.

God doesn't throne in some other world:
He came into this world
and has never left it.
Christ hasn't retired:
He's with us,
day in and day out.
At the Ascension, He didn't go away:
He disappeared.
We can't logically make a festival out of the Ascension
unless we appreciate the distinction
between departure and disappearance.
Departure causes an absence,
but disappearance inaugurates a hidden presence.
On Ascension day,
Christ became invisible,
was wholly glorified in His humanity
and began sharing His Father's infinite might.
Because of that, He's closer to each of us
than He ever was before.

Far from abandoning us and leaving us orphans,*
He acquired the very influence,
            the boundless efficacy,
      that enables Him to fill everything
            with His presence.ᵀ
We mustn't restrict Christ either to earth
                  or to heaven.
   His Ascension is,
         not a going up in space
                  that'd only separate us,
         but a going up in power
                  that intensifies His presence,
                        as the Eucharist proves.

Christ still remains the most active person
                  in the history of the world.
Saint Mark demonstrates that beyond a doubt
         in his narrative of the Ascension,
                  which begins,
      "Jesus was taken up into heaven,
         where He sits at the right hand of God."
We interrupt our reading and think,
      "It's all over:
               He's gone away,
                  and we've lost Him.
               He's sitting in glory up there, eternally,
                  while we wear ourselves out down here."
But Mark continues,
      "The Apostles went out and preached everywhere.
         And the Lord worked with them,
                  endorsing their message

by the miracles that followed."[8]
How consoling to think
that He's here
on earth
with us
and will never leave us again,
because His spiritualized presence
is more intensive
and extensive
than His physical presence could
ever've been.
For our own greater good,
He went away visibly
so we could find Him present invisibly
any time,
anywhere.

Do we believe in the communion of saints?
Do we believe Christ wants to gather heaven and earth
into a single body,
beyond which there's nothing:
"to re-assemble all things in Christ,
both those in the heavens
and those on the earth—
all in Him"?[9]

We may—and must—earnestly wish for a world
where people'd love one another,
be united
and all enjoy God together.
We may—and must—desire

to see the world other than it is
but not run away to some other world.
How often we've sung things like
    "O dearest Mother, let me flee
    This exile land of misery:
    I fain would die and follow thee."
But Jesus commands,
    "Go teach all nations"
        (the world we're forever leaving
           in those wretched hymns of ours);
    "baptize them
      in the name of the Father
           and of the Son
           and of the Holy Spirit,
and show them how to practice
    everything I've commanded you.
And you'll see that I'm with you
      every single day
        till the end of time."[10]

While we're planning to fly to heaven,
    God comes down to earth.
        So where do we think we're going?
To quote more of that pious doggerel,
    "Heaven has paid a visit to earth."
No, it wasn't a visit,
           one of those quick, discreet sympathy calls
             we slip away from
               with an "I'll pray for you."
God has settled down here for good.
    The distinctive word the Gospels use

to describe His presence
is *manet:*
"He abides."

Where's the Father?
Up in His heaven?
Indeed, not!
He's with us permanently.
"If anyone loves Me,
My Father'll love him,
and We'll come to him
and make Our abode with him."[11]
Where's the Holy Spirit?
With us
and in us forever.[12]
And our dead—where are they?
In communion
and close relationship with us.
They all spend their time in heaven doing good on earth.
Where would they be if not with Christ?
What would they be doing if not what He does?
In that case,
when we welcome Christ,
we welcome them;
and in furthering His work,
we collaborate with them.

Let's stop dreaming of heaven
as a refuge
or hiding place,
a super vacation resort

well secluded behind clusters of stars,
　　where God sits on a throne
　　　　with all the ex-Christians who've retired
　　　　　　from the business of this vile world.
God's not "up there"
　　presiding over an assembly of canonized pensioners;
and we needn't expect,
　　　　as soon as we've drawn our last breath,
　　to have nothing more to do than polish our halos.
"I shall see her some sweet day.
The Queen of smiles with ne'er a frown
Will place upon my brow a crown
Wherewith I shall reign for aye."
　　Maybe,
　　　　but not till we've done all we could
　　　　　　to lead the last of the stray sheep
　　　　　　　　back into the fold.

Dying means finding ourselves
　　in the most favorable circumstances
　　　　for the continued spreading of God's kingdom on earth.
Dying means being cured of some of our weakness,
　　　　　　some of our inadequacy,
　　　　and being made perfectly adaptable,
　　　　　　　　active
　　　　　　　　and available
　　　　　　　　　to carry on this same work
　　　　　　with those who haven't yet reached that stage
　　　　　　　　because they're still on earth.
That's the communion of saints:
　　all of us, under the lead of Christ,

workng together toward one goal
day after day
till the end of time.

The Redemption always depends on the Incarnation,
on God's invasion of
the world.
And the Incarnation's permanent.
As Durwell writes,
"Christ has arisen in a mystical body."
His glorious humanity's become the head
of a vast organism;
His risen Body's distinct
but shareable
and communicable,
capable of subjecting
and incorporating
into itself
all who don't resist Him.[18]
This presence of Christ here below,
made universal and accessible,
is called the Church.

For us, heaven signifies
starting to believe in His presence
and detect it,
starting to get used to it
and work to broaden it.
Faith's already a beginning of vision,
and charity's a theological virtue

in the full sense of the word
whether we're showing love to God
or to our neighbor.

There's what's new about our Lord's command.
If we want to see what our religious instruction's worth,
we just have to ask this simple question:
"What's this 'new commandment'?
What's new about it?"
Those who think they're well informed will answer,
"Love one another."
They're not exactly right.
That isn't what's new about it.
The precept itself already existed
in the Old Testament.
Christ merely summarized and quoted it,
and the Scribes approved.[14]
His real innovation consisted
in making the second commandment
identical with the first.
Since He became flesh,
brotherly love is theological.
If we love God,
we must love our brother;
and if we say we love God,
whom we don't see,
but refuse to love our brother,
whom we do see,
then we're liars.[15]
Our behaviour toward our neighbor
reveals our true attitude toward God.

To love our brother sincerely is to love God—
        but that's a bit of heaven,
            right now, on earth!
As a matter of fact, this world has to become heaven.
        Indeed, we pray for God's will to be done "on earth
            as it is in heaven";
        and if our plea isn't heard,
            that's only because we're lazy,
                            unbelieving
                            and fainthearted.

        The object of our prayer
            should also be the object of our faith and hope.
        Instead of running away from this world
            to reach heaven at length,
        we have to make it our business
            that God's will be done here on earth
                as it is in heaven.
Way down deep, we think, "That'll never happen."
        Well, then, why bother praying?
                So God'll do it?
        He wants it with all His might.
        The only obstacle is ourselves!
Because the victory depends partly on us,
        it isn't absolutely certain.
The world could end with something less
            than total redemption,
        but only because Gods' Redemption's
                been blocked—
            blocked by our refusal to
                    believe in His power,

serve
and redouble it.

Do we love God up in His heaven?
Do we look up at the starry sky to speak to Him?
    We should look closer:
        He's here, somewhere, beside us—
                perhaps gazing at the stars, like us,
                        because they're beautiful,
                or perhaps so hungry, cold and sick
                        He hasn't the strength to raise His head;
            and unless we hurry to feed and warm and
                        comfort Him,
                we'll miss God—
                        miss Him royally.
    "But, Lord, when did we see You like that?"[16]

According to our religion, God's become man.
    We can't be sure we're in tune with God
            unless we're in tune with our neighbor;
    we're no closer to God
            than we are to that neighbor.
Saint Matthew's version of the last judgment[17] shows
        that religious instruction will always fall short
                of convincing us.
    There, good and bad alike get the shock of their lives:
        at that moment, they discover—the Incarnation!
Good and bad alike learn, as if for the first time,
        that God was their neighbor,
        that the first and the second commandment

were one and the same,
that the first was fulfilled in the second
and that heaven'd begun on earth.

But we find it far less convenient that way.
As far as God goes,
it's relatively easy to love Him—
or to think we do.
We invent Him,
dream Him up,
style Him just the way we like:
when we're blue,
we make a bosom friend of Him;
when content,
we send Him packing;
we modify His features
according to the "inspiration" of the moment,
so that He ends up looking like us.
As Voltaire put it,
"God created men in His image and likeness,
and they've certainly turned the tables on Him."
For instance, Chateaubriand,
that inveterate egoist
who never gave his wife a thought,
described God as
"the Eternal Celibate of the worlds."
No need to ask where he got that notion.

If people tell us, "I love God,"
we should withhold our judgment
and hesitate to canonize them.

Perhaps they're merely going through a pious phase.
But if they say, "I love my neighbor,"
    then we can begin to esteem them
        as extraordinary beings.
        Perhaps we've met someone, at last,
                who can put up with God.

So we love God up in His heaven, do we?
    That means we love nothing—
            just a figment of our imagination.
    It'd be only too easy to "attain salvation"
                and "earn heaven"
        if all we had to do was spend half an hour a week
            shuffling around in some church
        "where, luckily, I don't know a soul."
No one feeds on Christ's flesh
    and no one's a naturalized citizen of heaven
        until,
            along with the host,
            he can swallow all his neighbors.
    There's a thought that makes it surprisingly easy to see
        how the Eucharist can be both a banquet
                and a sacrifice....

Communion means *common union.*
    The surest way to test the genuineness of our ecstasies
        is to adopt as our companions in heaven
            all our neighbors at Mass
                together with everything they've shown us so far.
    During thanksgiving,
        instead of screening them off from view

by burying our head in our hands,
we must be reconciled to the faces around us—
this "dear parishioner" on our right,
the pastor who just gave us Communion.
Saint John concludes,
"That's how we know we've passed from death to life:
because we love our brothers."[18]
That's also how we know heaven!

Christianity even gives brotherly love a sort of priority
over love of God.
"If you're in church
about to present your gift at the altar,
and you remember
your brother has a grievance against you,
leave your offering there
and, first, go make peace with him."[19]
We're to leave the altar,
our prayers,
our Mass,
our "heavenward flight"—
everything—
in order to seek out the brother we've grown away from.
And if we find it in our heart to love him again,
we'll also find heaven once more.

God and our neighbor are indissolubly linked.
But, oh, what trouble we have believing that!
If only God were enthroned high above
(as we try to convince ourselves),
good and far from us,

behind clouds of incense
and well bolted in His Paradise,
we wouldn't have to worry:
we could detest our neighbor without fear.

This is where Christian contemplation differs profoundly
from pagan contemplation.
Christians become contemplatives,
not to escape from this world
or "feel religion"
or enjoy ecstasies,
but to consider an incarnate God,
a crucified Saviour.
It's impossible to know and love God
without beginning to resemble Him;
and, for that reason, impossible to remain a contemplative
without becoming a missionary.
Saint Thérèse of the Child Jesus has been declared
patroness of the missions.

We needn't invent God,
but just accept Him as He reveals Himself;
we needn't go discover Him in the next world,
"where He's hiding,"
but just recognize Him in this world,
where He manifests Himself to those
who love Him.

And all those who *have* recognized Him
He's immediately sent back to their neighbors.
Fashioning them after His own heart,

He's always made missionaries of them.
To everyone who saw and knew the risen Christ—
                to Mary Magdalene,
                to the disciples from Emmaus,
                to Peter—
He commanded,
        "Go to My brothers . . ."[20]
        "Feed My lambs."[21]

Charles de Foucauld used to say that,
                for the kingdom of Christ,
        he was ready to go to the four corners of the earth
                        and live till the end of the world.
Those are the exact dimensions of Christ's missionary love:
        "Preach the Gospel to all nations"
                and
        "I'm with you constantly till time runs out."[22]
An authentic contemplative,
        Charles de Foucauld became a missionary
                like the God he'd looked upon;
        he placed himself so completely at God's disposal
                that the Love which saves the world
                        shone through him unimpeded.
"God has so loved the world!"[23]
We don't really share His thoughts
        unless we, too, love this earth
                        and everything in it,
        unless we're sorry we can't pray and work here
                till it's wholly stirred up,
                        consecrated
                                and imbued with love and joy.

When Christ refused to pray for the world,
 He didn't mean this earth as a whole
   but only those forces in it
    that resist God's activity.
The world He condemned is the one Satan rules over:
  the domain of egocentric isolationists
   who ex-communicate themselves
    from God and neighbor.
The boundary between that world
     and the one "God has so loved"
   passes through each of us;
 and it's up to us to push it back
     and add all we can to God's realm.

Everything we save from this world
  will be eternalized in heaven.
The Mass is this daily Pasch,
   this continual passing over
    from the profane to the sacred,
    from earth to heaven.
We mustn't allow anything to be lost
   or leave anything to be desecrated.
"The universe eagerly longs to see the sons of God,
  hoping to be liberated,
    like them,
    from its slavery to corruption,
   so as to share in the glorious freedom
    of God's children. . . .
 For we know that all creation groans
  with the pangs of birth."[26]
Are we burning to satisfy that expectation?

Too many Christians give up the world—
     at least, with regard to its salvation;
after getting all they can out of it,
     they doom it to destruction
          in the manner of the Apocalypse.
They should read more attentively.
Doesn't Saint Paul's text assert
          that heaven's brought forth here below?
The Apocalypse will reveal what already existed
          in a certain fashion
          and behind a veil.
The birth of a child's an apocalypse:
     the manifestation of a being
          who was already present
               but hidden.
There's nothing catastrophic about it,
     and the pains of labor are forgotten
          for joy that a man's born into the world.[25]
Harvest time's the apocalypse of the grain of wheat.
And isn't it primarily a festive season,
     even if it's also mowing time?
So, too, heaven'll be the joyous revelation
     of everything the love of God and His saints
          has brought to perfection in this world
               forever.

Everything we've really loved will be saved.
     Our redemptive power's proportionate
          to our capacity for love.
It's all a matter of loving something so much
     that we won't cast it aside.

People who "want to die as soon as possible"
                won't save anything.
    Creation'll be transfigured
        by sharing in the glorious freedom of the sons of God;
    and to the extent they ignore it
                to "save their souls,"
            they hinder the rebirth of the world.

God has willed to need us.
    He wants us, not merely to wait and wish for heaven,
                but to build it now
                    by starting to make this earth
                        a place where justice rules
                            and where we love
                                one another.
    We mustn't imagine that God'll surprise us
        with a prefabricated heaven of His own making
            to replace the one we're working on.

We couldn't validly choose our eternal destiny
    unless we'd already had a foretaste of it,
                after a fashion,
                even in this life.
"Test yourselves," Saint Paul urges.
        "Don't you know Christ is in you?"[26]
    Haven't we ever sensed heaven—
                                the kingdom of God—
                within us?
    Don't we ever notice this miracle:
        that,
                selfish and gruff,

mean and sarcastic as we are,
grace's taught us
to love
(sometimes for good),
to trust others,
to forget the wrongs we've suffered,
to give generously,
to be moved
if a persecutor of ours comes to grief,
touched
if he repents
and overjoyed
if he mends his ways?
Heaven's the only place
where there's more happiness over one sinner
who repents
than over a thousand men who don't need to.[27]
If we've felt the same way,
it's because we were in heaven at that moment;
it's because there *is* a heaven
and we have access to it.

As for hell—
the counterproof of heaven—
we have a preview of that, too:
the unbearable heaviness that comes over us
when disagreements and grudges cut us off
from the world where people love one another,
share,
believe

and tolerate
anything.
The gloom of our occasional eclipses
bears painful witness
to the habitual existence of a light
that must eventually shine through us
unobstructed.
If we're so chilled
and so uncomfortable
when we turn back into our "natural" selves.
individualistic and aloof,
conceited, independent—and desperate,
we should conclude
that it's become necessary for us
to be supernatural,
that we were made for another kind of life:
the life of heaven.

Heaven isn't a place,
but a state.
Passing from this world to heaven
doesn't entail moving from one location to another,
but turning toward God
and opening our hearts
to the things He continually wants to do
in us
and through us.
Because of sin,
God's kingdom and ours became two different worlds,
but they've established contact

and set up ceaseless relations,
and all our efforts and hopes should go
to bringing them closer, bit by bit.
till they finally merge into one.
Ever since His conversations with Adam,
God hasn't stopped frequenting mankind
and living on earth.
He speaks His reassuring "I'll be at your side"[28]
to all those
who want to draw near Him
and "walk in His presence"[29]—
from Abraham,
through all the prophets
down to the last Christian
at the end of the world.
"His name'll be Emmanuel."[30]
"He'll be with them as their God."[31]

There's a continual epiphany inherent in this world of ours—
a constant manifestation.
Man's been made capable of God,
and the earth susceptible of consecration
and sacrifice
(that is, of being made sacred).
Our terrestrial world has access to the celestial
whenever there's love,
giving,
communion.
For that reason,
the expression "gaining heaven" becomes not only false
but absurd,

and the charge of being mercenary refutes itself.
We don't gain heaven;
we get used to it,
grow accustomed to it,
acclimate ourselves to it,
train for it
and build it—
all of us together.

Heaven's the home of a reality
we most often see only the reverse side of;
it's the long-sought coincidence
between what we wished to be
and what we are;
it's taking full part, at last, in the procession
we could never quite keep step with;
it's a family
where we love each other,
where we laugh
and forever leap with joy
because we're together
because we can sing together
and always share in the
beatitudes
of the God who established it.
We have it in our power
to be in heaven with Him right away,
to be happy with Him at this very moment.
But being happy with Him
means being happy with His own happiness,
and that, in turn, means loving,

                                    helping,
                                    giving
                                         (giving our
                                              very life),
                                    rescuing
                                    and redeeming.
          Being "of heaven" rather than of this earth
               presupposes that we choose to serve
                         on the relief squad
                              instead of the leisure-time committee.

The world's been compared to a submarine
               that lies damaged on the ocean floor.
     Since the vessel's absolutely watertight,
          the crew members are alive
                              and can hope to be saved.
     Soon, they form two groups:
          one, to study means of resurfacing;
          and the other, to plan the details of everyday life.
     The first tries to make spare parts
                    and devises signals to contact other ships at sea;
          full of expectation,
               they're on the watch,
                    all ears
                         and straining toward life on the outside.
     The second schedules meals,
                              projects,
                              work periods
                              and entertainment.
     But, before long, the second group shouts to the first,
          "You dreamers are wasting your time.

Come over here and help us.
We're working—and having fun.
At least, we're accomplishing something."
Finally, the captain has to speak to everyone
and recall a basic fact:
"We're living inside this ship
just so we can get out.
We aren't meant to stay down here,
submerged in hate and thoughts of revenge,
in self-seeking and indifference,
in peace and security.
We're made for something else,
for an altogether different life.
Some've got so used to puttering around down here
that they don't think of resurfacing any more
and don't even care to."

How about us?
Do we want to go back up
and live once again
in a world where people converse,
where they know and love one another
and are interested
in what happens to
everybody,
where they're all bound together
in fellowship
and stay close to the one Source
of their fatherhood
and brotherhood,
where they throw themselves,

[279]

body and soul,
into all the work and all the joy
that waits for them?

Instead of that,
aren't we especially interested
in making our stay here below
as peaceful and comfortable as we can,
and in so improving our situation in the world
that,
besides enjoying the most modern
conveniences,
we can manage moments of asceticism
favorable to meditation
and the loftiest
transports?

Saint Peter reminds us we're "strangers and pilgrims" here.[32]
Those who believe
God still has work for them to do farther on
keep themselves ready, willing and able.
The saints are more vibrantly alive than anyone else,
more adaptable to any situation,
because they've detached themselves from everything
and, so, are free to embrace anything.

Those who don't feel perfectly content anywhere
are the only ones who can be happy everywhere,
the only ones who can work at every job
with the same prompt enthusiasm.
Because a saint isn't rooted to any one place,
he never looks as if he's been transplanted.

Because he doesn't see enough love anywhere,
      his grief impels him to love with all his might.
"Your sorrow will be changed into joy."[33]
Is that what our Lord meant?
    "When you find a want,
        you'll try to fill it
            and give more and more
                till you eventually give yourselves.
      Then you'll become a gift;
        you'll become love,
            joy
            and heirs of heaven."

Our life on earth'll be radiant and full,
                harmonious and happy,
  insofar as we believe
    that what it represents—
      what it announces,
      what it signifies—
    is infinitely more beautiful
        than what meets the eye;
  insofar as we believe
    that what visibly miscarried today
      is an invisible promise for tomorrow,
        because of the hope we put into it,
        because we know
          that ours is "a hidden life
            with Christ
              in God."[34]

We've all observed

that our deepest joys here below
　　always slip away
　　　　　before we realize it,
don't measure up,
　　　　to what we anticipated,
and yet, in retrospect, prove richer
　　　　than we were able to appreciate.
Newman once wrote
　　that the religious services
　　　　　which sickness, care and turmoil
　　　　　　　keep us from relishing;
　　those that weary our fickle heart
　　　　though they're actually being celebrated
　　　　and though we believe in their sacredness;
　　those that we're inclined to judge too long,
　　　　that we dread
　　　　　　before they begin
　　　　　　and wish to see done
　　　　　　　while they're still going on—
　　those very services,
　　　　we understand later,
　　are filled with the presence of God.
How can we be so blind to our supreme good!
　　We rush out,
　　　　inhale the first breath of fresh air
　　　　　　with avidity
　　　　　　and relief;
　　and then, in a flash, we realize
　　　　what we're missing,
　　　　what we're turning our back on,
　　and we know we were never happier

than the whole time we felt so bored.
We doze off,
        like Jacob in exile.
He lay down in the darkness of night
                with a stone for a pillow;
        but when he awoke
                and recalled what'd happened,
        he remembered
                that he'd seen angels
                        and the Lord,
                who manifested Himself through them.

We're so rarely the person we want to be. . . .
    The fact is
            we can't be our real selves except through grace.
        It takes a kind of state of grace
                for our faculties to work without hindrance
                and for us to be free to use what's most truly ours.
    Everything is grace:
        we come upon truth
                only by surprise;
        we speak it aptly
                only because we hit on the right words;
        we discover ourselves
                only when we give ourselves.
    Nothing short of death
        can definitively unlock to us
                the full expanse of our soul.

"Before going to bed at night," says Jacques Rivière,
        "we cast a tired look upon our day

and find something wanting in all our acts,
a discrepancy
between what we've done
and what we
resolved to do.
Not that we've spared ourselves:
we've worked steadily till bedtime—
all business,
each minute filled to bursting.
And yet we feel as if we've failed somehow,
though there was nothing we could do about it.
In fact, no matter what we try,
there's something slightly but consistently wrong
about all we do:
we never quite reach the goal;
there's always that strange moment
when the idea we were pursuing
slips away and vanishes;
and when we do finish a job,
the original concept stands a little farther off
and taunts us,
and all we have to show for our trouble
is a garbled image
of what we set out to do.
We're like people trying to regain an ancient title
long since lost.
All our activity's like those lumbering waves of memory
that come crashing against a wall of forgetfulness
and vanish in a mist.
We never "get it" just right.
A tree grows because it remembers.

From its deepest roots,
    it yearns to go back to its primitive form
       and seems likely to succeed.
But no, these aren't the gorgeous flowers
       it hoped to produce;
    and, as they fall,
       it stubbornly takes up the same dream,
           the same dark
              quest again.

And I—
    quite near
      and wholly interior,
    hardly distant from what I am,
      yet inaccessible till death—
I see,
I touch my soul:
    the soul I've fallen away **from**
        and can just vaguely imitate. . . .
  There's always a subtle,
       discouraging difference
          between ourselves
            and our soul."

In all we do,
    we're seeking a certain indefinite quality,
      an impression
        we've experienced only in passing.
At some time, perhaps,
    a book thrilled us,
    a meeting stirred us up,
    a saying or a piece of music shed light on everything.

From that moment on,
    each phase of our life seemed luminous;
    each part of our being could breathe deeply;
    we felt refreshed, confident, free,
        ourselves again,
        integrated and unified;
    we were happy admiring a landscape
            or listening to a concert.
Why is it that, now,
        the same author,
        the same countryside
        and the same melody
    don't mean a thing to us any more?
Why doesn't the miracle happen again?

This is what I think heaven'll be:
    re-experiencing,
        in a blaze of light,
        the wonderful moments of our earthly existence.
At each step along the way, we'll stop short,
    astounded by God's generosity
    and ashamed of our past heedlessness.
Reliving a single instant
    will send us into raptures of joy and gratitude.
We'll see how beautiful the world was
    and how boorish we were
        to walk among all those marvels
           sour-faced and disappointed.
We'll realize that God did a thousand things to cheer us up
        at every minute of every hour—
        like a father who spreads treasures before his child

to get a smile out of him
and, for thanks, hears the greedy little tyrant
mutter,
"Gimme some more."

The biggest surprise about heaven'll be
that there's nothing new there.
When we wake up from this long sleep
and all its nightmares,
we'll find ourselves clasped in the same arms
that've always held us.
The glorious face that'll beam down on us
in tenderness and joy
will be the one we always sensed was watching over us
in our trials and sorrows,
though we refused to believe in it.
At long last,
we'll recognize the elusive but faithful friend
whose mysterious presence puzzled us.
We'll understand why we always dimly felt
that life was amazingly kind and favorable to us
and that our indifference
and incredulity
came from sheer wrongheadedness.
We'll be able to guess
what our nonbelieving friends realized
at the hour of death
and what often made it so bitter for them:
the knowledge that they were leaving,
for the first time
and forever,

a grace of presence,
a source of goodness,
a brazier of life and love
that warmed their life somewhat
but was never allowed to enkindle it.

In C. S. Lewis' view,
the world isn't a very well-defined place.
If we choose it for our final home,
instead of heaven,
we'll soon notice
that it's always been a hell.
If we situate it just under heaven,
we'll find out that,
ever since the first day,
it's been a part of heaven itself.
In other words,
if we want to establish ourselves permanently
in an unredeemed state,
we'll lose both heaven and earth.
But if we're willing to work here below
with heaven in our heart,
with an insatiable desire for love
and progress,
we're already in heaven.
Everything on earth suggests and speaks of heaven;
but it all becomes mute
if we seize it by the throat
to make it shout the name it simply murmurs.

We mustn't renounce either heaven

or earth.
We mustn't long for some other world
but desire to make this world other than it is.
We mustn't stop working
or hoping.
Some people hope in such a way
that they don't work any more;
and others work with so little hope
that they disclaim all that's best in man and in life.
There's a lot of truth in the saying
"We have to work
as if everything depended
on us
and hope
as if everything depended
on God."
Through our activity,
a redemption's effected that transcends us.

At the moment of His Ascension,
when the Apostles watched Jesus rise before them,
perfectly naturally
and with every right,
they grew aware—
for the first time, no doubt—
of their mysterious companion's true identity.
They started to understand
who Jesus was,
what He'd done for them
and how they'd received Him.
For three years

God had lived with them,
God had eaten at their table,
God had slept in their homes,
God had told them all about Himself—
and they'd never even thanked Him.
Now they saw how rude and thoughtless they'd been;
they saw everything they could've done for Him,
everything they could've said,
all the happiness they could've given Him.
"And they stood there, gazing up into heaven."[35]
Heaven'd begun thirty-three years before,
and they hadn't noticed.

But angels came to shake them,
rouse them from their nostalgia
and send them into the world,
where their Master was waiting
for them.
It wasn't too late, they realized.
Now they could do for men
all they were sorry they hadn't done for Christ.
Together, they'd renew the great Adventure
that'd never end.
They were going to live heaven on earth.

NOTES

Preface

[1] Matthew 13:52
[2] See the sermon of November 13, 1836, in *Parochial and Plain Sermons*, IV, pp. 273–275, 277–279
[3] I Corinthians 3:10; John 4:37–38
[4] Deuteronomy 8:3; Matthew 4:4
[5] Psalms 42:3–4
[6] John 6:61

1. Is God Really Silent?

[1] Matthew 25:35
[2] Matthew 28:20
[3] Matthew 11:6
[4] Luke 23:34
[5] John 1:26
[6] John 14:9
[7] John 19:26
[8] John 8:47
[9] John 1:11
[10] John 3:19
[11] John 1:5
[12] John 1:46
[13] Acts 7:60, 8:3
[14] Acts 9:5
[15] John 14:9
[16] Luke 15:11–32
[17] Genesis 3:9
[18] Apocalypse 3:20
[19] Paul Claudel, *Positions et Propositions*, II.
[20] Matthew 17:1–8; Mark 9:1–7; Luke 9:28–36
[21] Matthew 17:4
[22] John 1:26

2. God's Word Is a Living Thing

[1] Hebrews 4:12
[2] John 1:9
[3] Matthew 8:8
[4] I John 4:16
[5] Genesis 3:8–11
[6] John 1:11
[7] Exodus 33:11
[8] Hebrews 1:1
[9] John 14:26
[10] Osee 2:16
[11] I Corinthians 2:9; Isaias 64:4
[12] Hebrews 4:12
[13] Luke 11:28
[14] Jeremias 35:15
[15] John 8:47
[16] Luke 10:22

[17] Genesis 12:1
[18] Exodus 33:20
[19] John 21:12
[20] Luke 8:43–48
[21] Luke 6:19
[22] Luke 24:27
[23] Colossians 2:17
[24] Luke 3:22
[25] I Corinthians 10:1–6
[26] I Corinthians 10:11
[27] John 16:25
[28] Hebrews 4:12–13
[29] Luke 5:8
[30] James 1:23–24
[31] John 1:5
[32] Luke 23:34
[33] Matthew 26:33–35
[34] I Samuel 24:5–6, 18
[35] II Samuel 11:2–12:13
[36] Matthew 24:46
[37] John 8:47
[38] John 3:19
[39] John 10:4
[40] Isaias 55:10–12
[41] John 4:13
[42] John 4:42

3. *Fortunate Are the Poor*

[1] John 15:12
[2] Matthew 5:3
[3] Luke 18:11
[4] Matthew 5:3
[5] Hebrews 11:8
[6] *Commentary on the Letter to the Hebrews*
[7] Luke 10:22
[8] *Ibid.*
[9] John 1:9
[10] Philippians 2:5–8
[11] John 10:17–18
[12] Hebrews 11:8
[13] Matthew 5:3
[14] Acts 1:6
[15] Matthew 5:5
[16] Matthew 11:21, 23:37; Luke 13:34
[17] John 15:11
[18] II Corinthians 7:9–11
[19] Matthew 5:4
[20] Matthew 5:6
[21] Matthew 8:20; Luke 9:58
[22] Psalms 41:4
[23] Matthew 5:7
[24] Matthew 5:40
[25] Matthew 5:46–48; Luke 6:32–36
[26] Genesis 3:9
[27] Matthew 5:9
[28] John 14:27
[29] Matthew 5:10
[30] Luke 6:23
[31] Matthew 5:12
[32] *Ibid.*
[33] John 17:10
[34] Matthew 11:6
[35] Matthew 11:3
[36] John 6:68
[37] Luke 1:53
[38] Luke 1:46–55

4. *God Is Love*

[1] I John 4:16
[2] John 18:17

[8] John 4:35
[4] Matthew 13:1
[5] John 4:8–15
[6] John 15:1
[7] John 6:35
[8] Luke 11:13
[9] Luke 10:22
[10] John 14:6
[11] John 10:8
[12] Mark 9:35
[13] Luke 21:1–4
[14] Luke 19:1–10
[15] Luke 1:44
[16] Luke 4:35
[17] Luke 7:36–50
[18] Luke 7:47
[19] John 10:3, 14
[20] John 8:47
[21] John 20:15–16
[22] John 21:4

[23] Luke 24:32
[24] Luke 24:35
[25] Luke 24:29
[26] John 10:17–18
[27] John 7:46
[28] Luke 2:51
[29] Luke 1:49
[30] John 15:16
[31] Luke 21:18
[32] Ephesians 3:18
[33] *The Problem of Pain* (New York: The Macmillan Co., 1948), pp. 55–56
[34] Mark 16:14
[35] John 5:17
[36] Luke 7:47
[37] I John 4:7
[38] John 10:3, 14
[39] John 15:12

5. *Forgiveness*

[1] Collect for the Tenth Sunday after Pentecost
[2] Romans 5:20
[3] Luke 5:32
[4] Luke 15:7
[5] Mark 2:7
[6] Luke 5:27–29
[7] Mark 2:15
[8] Luke 5:31
[9] Matthew 9:13
[10] *The Problem of Pain*, pp. 49–50

[11] John 16:8
[12] Luke 5:32
[13] Acts 26:14
[14] John 12:31
[15] Luke 14:10
[16] Matthew 8:20
[17] Luke 19:8
[18] Galatians 2:20
[19] Romans 7:15–24 *passim*
[20] Luke 5:32
[21] Psalms 41:6
[22] John 8:2–11

6. *The Holy Spirit*

[1] John 16:7
[2] Matthew 28:20
[3] John 16:7, 13

[4] Romans 8:15
[5] Collect for Pentecost
[6] Acts 19:2

7 Romans 8:9–14
8 John 14:12
9 John 4:10
10 *Veni, Creator Spiritus*
11 Hebrews 1:1
12 Matthew 21:35–37
13 John 14:9
14 Romans 8:15
15 John 18:23
16 John 18:21
17 Matthew 24:31
18 Ephesians 4:30–32, 5:2
19 Romans 8:14
20 Matthew 18:20
21 Ezechiel 37:1–14
22 Acts 2:6
23 Luke 9:55
24 Genesis 1:27
25 Matthew 5:23–24
26 Matthew 25:40
27 John 13:34
28 Leviticus 19:18
29 Mark 12:31

30 Matthew 25:40
31 I John 4:7
32 Matthew 7:21
33 Matthew 25:31–46
34 John 5:17
35 Matthew 25:24–30
36 Luke 10:30–37
37 Luke 16:19–31
38 John 14:9
39 John 10:16
40 Luke 10:3
41 Hymn for the Second Vespers of Pentecost
42 Acts 10:44–48
43 John 20:17
44 John 21:17
45 Matthew 28:19
46 John 20:21
47 Luke 24:33–35
48 John 14:26
49 Ephesians 4:30
50 Romans 4:18
51 Alleluia verse for Pentecost

7. *Lay Spirituality*

1 Acts 9:16
2 Mark 5:1–20
3 Luke 10:42
4 Matthew 24:45
5 John 14:12
6 John 20:21
7 Matthew 28:7
8 John 3:16
9 John 17:15

10 Matthew 3:17
11 Romans 8:32
12 John 5:17
13 John 14:31
14 Ephesians 1:3–6
15 John 8:29
16 John 5:36
17 John 15:10–11

8. *The Lord's Handmaid*

1 John 1:14
2 Luke 1:38
3 Luke 1:38–39

4 Luke 22:42
5 Genesis 15:2–18:15, 21:1–21
6 Luke 2:51

[7] Matthew 8:8
[8] Luke 1:50–54
[9] Isaias 55:9
[10] Luke 1:18–22
[11] Matthew 11:5; Luke 7:22
[12] Luke 1:32–33, 37
[13] Luke 2:49
[14] Luke 2:41–50
[15] John 2:4

[16] Matthew 12:47–50
[17] Luke 11:27
[18] Luke 8:21
[19] Matthew 27:46
[20] John 15:8
[21] John 14:12
[22] Luke 1:45
[23] Luke 1:48–49

9. Heaven

[1] Luke 10:9
[2] I Corinthians 3:9; II Corinthians 6:1
[3] John 17:3
[4] John 1:9
[5] Romans 8:21
[6] John 14:18
[7] Ephesians 4:10
[8] Mark 16:20
[9] Ephesians 1:10
[10] Matthew 28:20
[11] John 14:23
[12] John 14:17
[13] Philippians 3:21
[14] Matthew 22:36–40; Luke 10:25–27
[15] I John 4:20
[16] Matthew 25:44
[17] Matthew 25:31–46

[18] I John 3:14
[19] Matthew 5:23–24
[20] Matthew 28:7
[21] John 21:15
[22] Matthew 28:19–20
[23] John 3:16
[24] Romans 8:19–22
[25] John 16:21
[26] II Corinthians 13:5
[27] Luke 15:7
[28] Judges 6:16
[29] Genesis 17:1
[30] Isaias 7:14
[31] Apocalypse 21:3
[32] I Peter 2:11
[33] John 16:20
[34] Colossians 3:1–4
[35] Acts 1:10